guided writing INSTRUCTION

STRATEGIES TO HELP STUDENTS BECOME BETTER WRITERS

SHELLEY PETERSON

PORTAGE &
MAIN PRESS

© 2003 Shelley Peterson

Portage and Main Press acknowledges the financial support of the Government of Canada through the Book Publishing Industry Development (BPIDP) for our publishing activities.

All rights reserved. Except as noted, no part of this publication may be reproduced or transmitted in any form or by any means—graphic, electronic, or otherwise—without the prior written permission of the publisher.

Printed and bound in Canada by Hignell Book Printing
Book and cover design: Gallant Desgin Ltd.

03 04 05 06 07 5 4 3 2 1
National Library of Canada Cataloguing in Publication

Peterson, Shelley Lynn, 1961-
      Guided writing instruction: strategies to help students become better writers / Shelley Peterson.

Includes bibliographical references.
ISBN 1-55379-018-9

     1. English language--Writing--Study and teaching. 2. English language--Writing. 3. English language--Rhetoric. I. Title.

PE1408.P47 2003   808'.042   C2003-905822-0

PORTAGE & MAIN PRESS

100-318 McDermot Avenue
Winnipeg, Manitoba Canada R3A 0A2
Toll free: 1-800-667-9673
Fax: 1-866-734-8477
Website: www.portageandmainpress.com

Table of Contents

Chapter 1: Teaching and Assessing Writing
Teaching Writing 1
    Students Establish Purposes for their Writing 2
    Establishing Author Groups 2
    Peer Conferencing 2
    Student-Teacher Conferences 3
    Finding 'Real' Audiences for Students' Writing 3
    Teachers Writing with Students 3
    Recognizing Students' Personal Writing Processes 3
    Recognizing Social and Cultural Influences on Writing 4
Schedule for a Typical 30-60 Minute Writing Class 5
Assessing Writing 5
References 14

Chapter 2: Gathering Ideas for Writing 15
Fiction 15
    Generating Ideas for Fiction Writing 16
    Alternatives to Story Starters 16
        Mini-Lesson: Creating an Idea Bank: Personal Experiences 16
        Mini-Lesson: Creating an Idea Bank: Realistic and Historical Fiction 21
        Mini-Lesson: Creating an Idea Bank: Fantasy 26
Nonfiction 31
        Mini-Lesson: Generating Topics to Achieve Many Purposes 33
        Mini-Lesson: Narrowing the Focus 38
References 41

Chapter 3: Fiction—Character Development   43
    Characters are Integral to a Good Story   43
    Gender Stereotypes   43
       Mini-Lesson: Observing Others to Create Characters for Stories   45
       Mini-Lesson: Character Development   48
       Mini-Lesson: Developing Characters Using Dialogue   51
References   54

Chapter 4: Developing and Organizing Ideas   55
Fiction   55
    Different Ways of Telling Stories   55
       Mini-Lesson: Creating Captivating Leads: Using Different Approaches   56
       Mini-Lesson: Generating Possible Story Lines   61
Nonfiction   63
       Mini-Lesson: Writing Effective Leads   63
       Mini-Lesson: Organizing Ideas and Using Headings   69
       Mini-Lesson: Writing Using Paragraphs   72
References   75

Chapter 5: Description and Detail   77
Fiction   77
       Mini-Lesson: Using Specific Words and Phrases   78
       Mini-Lesson: Using Strong Verbs   82
Nonfiction   85
       Mini-Lesson: Giving Concrete Details to Support Big Ideas   86
       Mini-Lesson: Using Description   89
References   92

Chapter 6: Teaching Writing Conventions and Editing Skills   93
    Frequently Asked Questions about Classroom Editing   94
    Guiding Students' Editing: Student-Teacher Editing Conferences   95
       Mini-Lesson: Using Editing Symbols   98
    Using Inductive Teaching, Look for Patterns across Specific Examples   102
       Mini-Lesson: Punctuating Dialogue   102
    Using Deductive Teaching, Learning the Rules and Finding Examples   105
       Mini-Lesson: Capitalization Rules   105
       Mini-Lesson: Identifying and Transforming Sentence Fragments   113
References   118

CHAPTER 1

Teaching and Assessing Writing

TEACHING WRITING

In many ways, whenever we use books as models of effective writing in the classroom, the books and their authors become our 'co-teachers.' Our classroom libraries are filled with on-demand 'team teachers.' Books and their authors help illustrate ways for students to: develop characters, captivate the interest of readers through foreshadowing, use specific language to create an image, or use conventional punctuation and spelling to communicate ideas more clearly. We use ideas and techniques of other 'teachers' to help our students become better writers every time we use published literature in our writing lessons.

The teaching ideas in this book are based on a belief that our students become better writers through guided instruction and self-assessment. Vygotsky's theory of proximal development (1978)—that novice learners can develop skills and concepts more readily with the guidance of someone who is more competent and has more knowledge—supports this belief. Students learn from authors through the use of published material, and then use the new knowledge in their own writing. Students also work with their teachers to develop and apply assessment criteria based on this type of learning.

Guided instruction and assessment ideas in this book integrate easily into process writing classrooms (Calkins 1994; Graves 1994). A process writing classroom tends to be characterized by a number of elements such as:

- having students establish purposes for their writing
- establishing author groups
- peer conferencing
- student-teacher conferencing
- finding 'real' audiences for students' writing
- teachers writing with students
- recognizing students' personal writing processes
- recognizing social and cultural influences on student writing

Students Establish Purposes for Their Writing

Writing instruction and assessment work together to enhance students' self-confidence and abilities to use writing to achieve a number of social purposes (Halliday 1975). Students may write to:

- inform (e.g., reports, notes)
- entertain by creating imaginative worlds (e.g., poems, stories, anecdotes, jokes)
- develop questioning skills (e.g., letters of inquiry, information gathering, questionnaires)
- persuade (e.g., letters to the editor, advertisements, editorials)
- develop relationships with others (e.g., letters, e-mail correspondence)
- manage the writer's own behaviour, or the behaviour of others (e.g., class rules, to-do lists)
- come to know themselves (e.g., diaries, poems)

In order to accomplish these purposes, students need opportunities to make decisions about the topic, format, and audience for their writing.

Establishing Author Groups

In author groups with three or four members, students provide feedback about each other's writing. Ideally, author groups stay together for extended periods of time (perhaps 1-2 months) in order to build trusting relationships.

In these groups, students and the teacher (when it is appropriate) read drafts of each student's writing. Group members take turns describing characteristics of the writing that are effective and explain what is unclear, confusing, or needs to be revised.

Teachers may need to show students how to provide suggestions to the writer. Students often feel vulnerable when reading their written work to peers, so it is important for teachers to establish expectations and model respectful ways to make suggestions within the author groups. Researchers such as Timothy Lensmire (1994), Margaret Finders (1997), and Brett Elizabeth Blake (1997) provide ample evidence of the ways in which socially powerful students may use author groups and the content of their writing to hurt or silence their peers. Teachers need to ensure that all students understand the main goals of the feedback in an author group are to:

- enhance the student writers' self-confidence
- improve the effectiveness of a student's writing

Peer Conferencing

If classrooms are set up so students can talk to one another while they write, they can share their ideas with their peers and use these ideas in their writing. They can also receive ongoing feedback about how clearly they communicate their ideas and how their peers will accept their writing.

In my research (in press, 2003) in a grade-eight classroom, students asked questions and suggested ideas to peers seated in desks close to their own. Students explored ideas and drew in new information from peers to help them shape their thoughts and writing. Peer responses helped students gain a better idea of what was socially acceptable within the classroom's social structure. Questions about the plausibility of their writing were particularly powerful because the students were concerned about appearing foolish or naïve. The students had an opportunity to negotiate the social meanings of their writing in a less threatening small-group setting, saving them from potential embarrassment.

Student-Teacher Conferencing

In a student-teacher conference, conversation occurs between a student and a teacher. Before the conference, the teacher and students identify elements of the student's writing that need improvement. In a one-on-one conference of 5-10 minutes, these elements are discussed. Teachers may find it best to comment on more obvious aspects of the writing that need to be revised or edited, or they may choose to concentrate on specific aspects that have been addressed in other writing lessons.

Finding 'Real' Audiences for Students' Writing

Students may read their work aloud to the class, or they may choose to find another audience for their writing—relatives, students in another class, the local newspaper, and so on.

Teachers Writing with Students

Teachers show the value of writing by participating in the writing process with students and sharing the same joys and challenges. Trying to find topics and suitable formats for writing, deciding where to go next, and figuring out how to express an idea more clearly are all challenges that teachers can share with their students. Students will see that even though adults (their teacher, for instance) sometimes get frustrated with the writing process, adults still see writing as important and rewarding.

Recognizing Students' Personal Writing Processes

In many resources for teaching writing, a definitive model for *the* writing process is put forward as a way of understanding what writers do in order to produce a polished, publishable piece of writing. What is considered 'the writing process' usually involves some form of planning and thinking through of ideas prior to writing—either in the writer's head or on paper, brainstorming, or with lists, and so on—some initial drafting, further revision of the writing, and, finally, some editing before publication.

My own experiences as a writer and teacher have changed my thinking about the usefulness of a universal model of 'the writing process.' Indeed, in two previous books, *Becoming Better Writers*, and *Teaching Conventions Unconventionally*, I included my own version of a recursive, circular process for writing. I have participated in writing classes where I was chastised for revising as I wrote, rather than after completing a full rough draft. It was extremely frustrating to be chained to someone else's version of the processes writers should use. I did not take any pride or pleasure in the writing that came from that class. The process of writing is extremely personal, and though I know that my teacher experienced success using her process and that she was trying to help me by teaching me to use her approach, it was not necessarily the best method for me.

Published authors take different approaches to the writing process. Georgia Heard (1995, 32), for example, says: "As I walk I write. Words circle my head. I speak lines out loud to see how they'll sound. The rhythm of walking orders my mind and limbers me up for the hours I will sit in one place. When I finally do sit down to write, I've already been at it for an hour."

Any writing model is *a* presentation of a writing process, rather than *the* writing process. We must respect the idiosyncratic nature of writing and consider the possibility that the structures put in place for guiding our students to improve their writing may not be helpful to *all* students. Be sure to remain sensitive to the diversity in the classroom, and accept that there will be a number of different writing processes.

Recognizing Social and Cultural Influences on Writing

This book takes into account criticism that the process approach to writing has been interpreted in such a way that it ignores the written product and focuses almost exclusively on the process (Blake 2001; Dyson 1997; Gilbert 1993; Lensmire 2000). These researchers argue that a student's gender, first language, race, socio-economic status, ethnicity, religion, sexuality, and geographic location influence his/her writing. The kinds of writing that are valued in schools and the nature of writing instruction and assessment must be reconsidered so that all students in our diverse classrooms can become confident and competent writers. Teaching and assessment suggestions in this book bring process and product together in ways that honour social and cultural differences in our students, and help teachers teach and assess the writing of diverse groups of students.

SCHEDULE FOR A TYPICAL 30-60 MINUTE WRITING CLASS

15-20 minutes Independent writing and peer conferencing
Students read published writing and look for ideas.
Students think, plan, write, revise, edit, and so on.
Teacher circulates and informally conferences with individual students.

10-15 minutes Writing lesson
Lessons may be for small groups or the whole class, depending on students' needs.

15-20 minutes Author groups
While the rest of the class reads and/or writes, author groups meet for discussion sessions. These sessions may be scheduled by the teacher or they may arise as students indicate a need.

One member of the group reads part or all of an unpolished draft. Other group members provide feedback to assist the writer in revising or completing the piece.

5-10 minutes Sharing writing
In a small group setting, or as a class, students and the teacher read the final versions of the stories. The rest of the class provides positive feedback to the writer.

ASSESSING WRITING

The formidable challenges for teachers in the assessment process are:

1. How to assess in a way that helps students become better writers.
2. How to assess the writing in a fair and equitable way.

Assessment of writing is subjective. Every teacher brings a different set of values, experiences, and perspectives to assessing student writing. Because of the subjective nature of writing, it is important to incorporate student self-assessment techniques into the assessment process, and to assess many written products on an ongoing basis throughout the school year.

Teachers can reduce subjectivity in their assessment by gaining a better sense of the levels of writing students in other classes are achieving in the same grade-levels. Meeting with a colleague and comparing samples of student writing on a regular basis help teachers understand what level students are at, and what level they should be at. Teachers can see what other students can achieve and then compare to the students in their classrooms. This activity provides an element of professional development for teachers, and students benefit from having two teachers negotiate a mark for their writing.

Mountford (1999) argues that the criteria traditionally used to assess student writing tend to reflect the kind of writing that European, middle-class students—often girls—are more likely to produce. Research suggests that in reality the values and processes of writing come from diverse social and cultural groups, and these should be incorporated into the rubrics that teachers use to assess. This may mean that teachers choose to modify rubrics to reflect the storytelling styles, topics, and genres that are appropriate for each student in their classroom.

Three types of rubrics, with criteria that are traditionally used to assess students' narrative writing, are **analytic scales, holistic scoring guides,** and **primary trait scoring.**

Analytic scales address components of writing such as ideas, organization, use of language, and use of grammar and writing conventions. There is a score for each component.

Holistic scoring guides provide criteria for making overall judgments of the quality of a piece of writing.

Primary trait scoring focuses on one aspect of the writing that defines the major purpose that is achieved using a particular form of writing.

The following narrative paper (Fig. 1.1), written by a grade-six boy, would likely be scored as meeting grade-level expectations on a **holistic scoring guide** (Fig. 1.2). The characters are introduced effectively in the first two paragraphs through lively dialogue, and the setting and events are developed fairly effectively. There are some supporting details about the characters' actions, and coherence between the actions is generally maintained through the use of the dream that forewarns the protagonist. The ending could be better developed so readers' questions are addressed: What happened to the characters and why did they do what they did? Was Sarah inside the house reading the letters when the house burned down? The writer uses some specific language (e.g., "strolling" and "chuckled"). He uses simple, compound, and complex sentences correctly and uses correct spelling, grammar, and punctuation except for two types of errors that are repeated.

If the **analytic scales** (Fig. 1.3) were used to score the writing in figure 1.1, the paper would likely meet grade-level expectations in terms of content, organization, and vocabulary. It would likely score at the "exceeds grade-level expectations" for sentence structure and conventions because the errors are really only of two types—the misplaced commas in the dialogue and the spelling of "enormous" and "led." Otherwise, the writer consistently and correctly uses conventions.

It's 9:00 pm on October 31. My family and I were strolling down the road in our car. Jack and Tim, my little brothers, are goofing around and trading Pokemon cards. "Hey Sarah!" said my mom, Marianna, "Could you please close your window? It's getting chilly." "No!" yelled Sarah. Bob replied with an enormous yell, " Sarah, how dare you say that to your mother? After we get home, we're taking all your cash and giving it to your little brothers!" "Oh, and you're grounded." "Ching!!! Ching!!!", chuckled Tim and Jack. Sarah sighed and said, "Not only am I broke, I'm grounded too." "Okay, okay, Sarah, you can keep $20.00 and that's it," said Bob. "I'll go take a look", said Marianna. After she got out she saw something in the bushes. "Bob", said Marianna, "Come out here and take a look at the engine." "Okay, I'm coming honey." Just before he stepped out of the car he saw an enormous mansion up ahead. The rest of the family got out of the car and Bob lead the way towards the house.

"Mom," said Sarah, "Are we gonna sleep in that broken down shack?" "We probably will," said Marianna, "It's time you slept like a man". "But I don't wanna be a man," said Sarah. After they got in, they heard a rattle, "What's that?" asked Tim. "Probably just a chandelier," said Bob. He flicked on his lighter and looked on the floor. He saw a message in bloody letters. It said, don't disturb or you will DIE. "No!" yelled Sarah. They went upstairs and found 5 big rooms. "1 room for each," said Marianna. "Good night everybody," said Bob. At 12:00 am when Sarah woke up, she went to Tim's room to check on him. When she walked in, all she saw was a skull and more bones. Mom came in with a can of oil and poured it all over the floor. Then Bob came in and lit the room on fire. Sarah screamed and woke up. "It was only a silly dream," she sighed. Suddenly she heard a sound come from downstairs. "Everyone run!" yelled Sarah, but no one came out of their rooms. First Sarah went to check Tim's room and saw blood stains all over the room. "AAAHHHH!" she yelled. Her mom and dad ran out of their rooms. "Sarah, it's 12:09 am, go back to bed" said Marianna. Sarah got her dad's rifle that was in the car and went into the kitchen. Suddenly the floor opened underneath her and she fell onto a pile of hay, and she fell asleep, and 5 minutes later she woke up and saw someone with 2 screws through his ears. He looked like a Frankenstein.

The Frankenstein went up a hidden set of stairs. The staircase lead to the 5 rooms. There were 5 stairwells. He went up to the 5th room where dad was sleeping. Dad came walking down with a can of oil. Then Tim, Jack and mom came walking down with cans of oil. All of them poured oil all over the mansion. After dad got his lighter out, Sarah said to herself, "Maybe my dream was trying to warn me about this." He lit the lighter and dropped it. The room caught fire, Sarah saw a staircase and ran down it. It was the basement. She found old bones and a diary. She opened it and blue dust came out, but before she could even read the first word, the house burned down.

Fig. 1.1

Using a **holistic scoring guide** (Fig. 1.5) to assess the sixth-grade persuasive paper "Whose Land Is This Land?" (Fig. 1.4), note that the writer presents the issue by questioning why First Nations people are being forced to live on reserves. The author provides specific supporting details in a consistently effective way, using paragraphs to organize the information. The title leads us to believe that the paper will discuss the ownership of land, however, the body of the paper actually focuses on issues arising from living on First Nations' reserves. The main idea is clearly stated in the final paragraph and in the equations at the end of the paper. Connections between the supporting details and
the main idea would be helpful to readers. For example, providing background information on how living on reserves is connected to the First Nations children being separated from their families would be help clarify the paper. The author uses specific terms and expressions such as "readily accessible," and "sacred land." The writer uses simple and compound sentences, but there are a few complex sentences. One good example is: "The children should not be abused in school when they speak one word of their own language." The author uses questions effectively and appropriately. Punctuation and spelling are consistently correct, except for the misspelling of "destroying." Grammar is generally correct. Holistically, the paper would likely be scored as exceeding grade-level expectations.

If the persuasive paper were scored using an analytic scale (Fig. 1.6), it would likely be assessed as meeting grade-level expectations for content because the issue is clearly defined, and most of the paragraphs clearly develop the issue. The paragraphs are organized in a way that enhances the argument, and each paragraph introduces new information that supports the argument. The paper would likely be scored "exceeding grade-level expectations" for organization. It would likely be assessed as "exceeding grade-level expectations" for vocabulary, sentence structure, and writing conventions. This is based on the effective use of language, the variety of sentence structures, and the almost error-free use of conventions.

Holistic Scoring Guide for Narrative Writing (One Possibility)

Below grade-level expectations	Approaching grade-level expectations	Meets grade-level expectations	Exceeds grade-level expectations
Provides little information about characters, setting, and/or events	Introduces and shows little development of characters, setting, and/or events	Introduces and develops characters, setting, and events fairly effectively	Consistently and effectively introduces and develops characters, setting, and events
Provides general ideas with no supporting details	Provides a few specific supporting details	Provides some specific supporting details	Provides specific supporting details in a consistently effective way
Makes it difficult to see the connection between events, actions, and details	Includes events, actions, and details that do not seem connected	Generally maintains coherence between events, actions, and details	Consistently maintains coherence between events, actions, and details
Has no clear beginning, middle, or ending	Unevenly develops beginning, middle, and ending	Develops beginning, middle, and ending to some degree	Develops beginning, middle, and ending effectively, and ties everything together with a satisfying ending
Uses limited vocabulary, and may use language inappropriately	Uses general words and expressions	Uses some specific words and expressions	Uses specific words and expressions in a lively and effective way
Uses simple sentences only	Uses simple sentences primarily and a few compound sentences	Uses simple and compound sentences, and sometimes uses complex sentences	Uses a variety of simple, compound, and complex sentences
Consistently makes spelling, grammar, and punctuation errors that interfere with communication	Sometimes makes spelling, grammar, and punctuation errors that interfere with communication	Generally uses correct spelling, grammar, and punctuation	Consistently uses correct spelling, grammar, and punctuation

Fig. 1.2

Analytic Scale for Narrative Writing (One Possibility)

	Below grade-level expectations	Approaching grade-level expectations	Meets grade-level expectations	Exceeds grade-level expectations
Content	Provides little information about characters, setting, and/or events Provides general ideas with no supporting details	Introduces and shows little development of characters, setting, and/or events Provides a few specific supporting details	Introduces and develops characters, setting, and events fairly effectively Provides some specific supporting details	Effectively introduces and develops characters, setting, and events Provides specific supporting details consistently
Organization	Makes it difficult to see the connection between actions, events, and details	Includes events, actions, and details that do not seem connected	Generally maintains coherence between events, actions, and details	Consistently maintains coherence between events, actions, and details
Vocabulary	Has no clear beginning, middle, or ending Uses limited vocabulary, and may use language inappropriately	Unevenly develops beginning, middle, and ending Uses general words and expressions	Develops beginning, middle, and ending with one part that may seem contrived or thinly developed Uses some specific words and expression	Develops beginning, middle, and ending effectively, and ties everything together with a satisfying ending Uses specific words and expressions in a lively and effective way
Sentence Structure	Uses simple sentences only	Uses simple sentences, and sometimes uses compound sentences	Uses simple and compound sentences primarily, with the occasional complex sentence	Uses a variety of simple, compound, and complex sentences. Uses interrogative and exclamatory sentences for effect where appropriate
Conventions	Consistently makes spelling, grammar, and punctuation errors that interfere with communication	Sometimes makes spelling, grammar, and punctuation errors that interfere with communication	Generally uses correct spelling, grammar, and punctuation	Consistently uses correct spelling, grammar, and punctuation

Fig. 1.3

GUIDED WRITING: STRATEGIES TO HELP STUDENTS BECOME BETTER WRITERS

Whose Land Is This Land?

Today, many First Nations people live on reserves in Canada. First Nations people have lived in Canada for many many years. They have different cultures, beliefs and different traditions than many Canadians. The First Nations speak many different languages. But why is the Canadian gov't forcing First Nations people to live on reserves?

It was their land first, and the Canadians should not be ruling and trying to take all of it. What about the children? Their education, it is only second-rate. The children should not be abused in school when they speak one word of their own language. They should not be forced to learn English. The children should be able to speak their own language. The First Nations family should not be separated. They shouldn't have to hide their children just so the Canadians won't take them away.

However, according to Statistics Canada, the suicide rate for Native Canadians is estimated up to 3.3 times the national average. Living on reserves is killing the First Nations people. The First Nations should not be ruled by the Canadians. There would be less substance abuse and also off reserves we would give the Native children a chance for a better education.

But what if the First Nations people want to stay on reserves? Maybe they want to keep the traditions alive for more generations to come. Their ancestors could be buried on sacred land. The first Nations people probably want to teach their children traditional life and traditional beliefs. Living on reserves the First Nations would get tax breaks. Fishing and hunting are readily accessible and we would not be destroying the sacred ground/land that's there.

Native Canadians have more and better chances for better and an enjoyable life not living on reserves. The children will have a better education and health. They have a better chance for jobs. Living on reserves is killing the Natives!

No Reserves = A Better Life!
&
Reserves = Not such a good life!

Fig. 1.4

Holistic Rubric for Persuasive Writing (One Possibility)

Below grade-level expectations	Approaching grade-level expectations	Meets grade-level expectations	Exceeds grade-level expectations
Does not define the issue clearly	Defines the issue but loses focus in several places in the paper	Clearly defines the issue, and generally maintains the focus	Clearly defines the issue, and maintains the focus throughout the paper
Provides general ideas with no supporting details	Provides a few specific supporting details	Provides some specific supporting details	Provides specific supporting details in a consistently effective way
Has no clear overall structure or organization	Has some structure or organization	Organizes information appropriately	Organizes information in a way that enhances the argument
Uses limited vocabulary, and may use language inappropriately	Uses general words and expressions	Uses some specific words and expressions	Uses specific words and expressions in a lively and effective way
Uses simple sentences only	Uses simple sentences, and sometimes uses compound sentences	Uses simple and compound sentences primarily, and sometimes uses complex sentences	Uses a variety of simple, compound, and complex sentences.
Consistently makes spelling, grammar, and punctuation errors that interfere with communication	Sometimes makes spelling, grammar, and punctuation errors that interfere with communication	Generally uses correct spelling, grammar, and punctuation	Consistently uses correct spelling, grammar, and punctuation

Fig. 1.5

Analytic Rubric for Narrative Writing (One Possibility)

	Below grade-level expectations	Approaching grade-level expectations	Meets grade-level expectations	Exceeds grade-level expectations
Content	Does not define the issue clearly Provides general ideas with no supporting details	Defines the issue but loses focus in several places in the paper Provides a few specific supporting details	Clearly defines the issue, and generally maintains the focus Provides some specific supporting details	Clearly defines the issue and consistently maintains the focus Provides specific supporting details consistently
Organization	Has no clear overall structure or organization	Has some structure or organization	Organizes information appropriately	Organizes information in a way that enhances the argument
Vocabulary	Uses limited vocabulary, and may use language inappropriately	Uses general words and expressions	Uses some specific words and expressions	Uses specific words and expressions in a lively and effective way
Sentence Structure	Uses simple sentences only	Sometimes uses simple and compound sentences correctly	Uses simple and compound sentences correctly and sometimes uses complex sentences	Uses a variety of simple, compound, and complex sentences
Conventions	Consistently makes spelling, grammar, and punctuation errors that interfere with communication	Sometimes makes spelling, grammar, and punctuation errors that interfere with communication	Generally uses correct spelling, grammar, and punctuation	Consistently uses correct spelling, grammar, and punctuation

Fig. 1.6

REFERENCES

Blake, B. E. 1997. *She say, he say: Urban girls write their lives.* Albany, NY: SUNY Press.

Blake, B. E. 2001. Fruit of the devil: Writing and English language learners. *Language Arts,* 78(5), 435-441.

Calkins, L. M. 1994. *The art of teaching writing.* 2nd Edition. Portsmouth, NH: Heinemann.

Dyson, A. H. 1997. *Writing superheroes: Contemporary childhood, popular culture, and classroom literacy.* New York: Teachers College Press.

Finders, M. J. 1997. *Just girls: Hidden literacies and life in junior high.* Urbana, IL: NCTE.

Gilbert, P. 1993. A story that couldn't be read. In P. Gilbert (Ed.), *Gender stories and the language classroom* (pp. 11-36). Victoria, Australia: Deakin University Press.

Graves, D. 1994. *A fresh look at teaching writing.* Portsmouth, NH: Heinemann.

Halliday, M. A. K. 1975. *Learning how to mean.* New York: Elsevier North-Holland, Inc.

Heard, G. 1995. *Writing toward home: Tales and lessons to find your way.* Portsmouth, NH: Heinemann.

Lensmire, T. 1994. *When children write: Critical re-visions of the writing workshop.* New York: Teachers College Press.

Lensmire, T. 2000. *Powerful writing, responsible teaching.* New York: Teachers College Press.

Mountford, R. 1999. Let them experiment: Accommodating diverse discourse practices in large-scale writing assessment. In C. R. Cooper & L. Odell (Eds.), *Evaluating writing: The role of teachers' knowledge about text, learning, and culture.* (pp. 366-396). Urbana, IL: NCTE.

Peterson, S. 2003. Peer response and students' revisions of their narrative writing. *L-1 Literacy.*

Vygotsky, L. S. 1978. *Mind in society: The development of higher psychological processes.* Cambridge, MA: Harvard University Press.

CHAPTER 2

Gathering Ideas for Writing

FICTION

"What is important to me?" This is the main question we want students to ask themselves to help gather ideas for their fiction writing. Often students feel a desire to write when they are passionate about a topic or idea, or when they want to communicate with particular readers. Also, having a strong desire to fulfill a particular purpose and wanting to try out a particular genre are good reasons for students to write (Wood Ray 1999). As teachers, we must support students in coming up with topics and ideas for their writing. We help students see that good writing comes from awakening what is extraordinary in our everyday lives.

> Writers live twice. They go along with their regular life, are as fast as anyone in the grocery store, crossing the street, getting dressed for work in the morning. But there's another part of them that they have been training. The one that lives everything a second time. That sits down and sees their life again and goes over it. Looks at the texture and details. (Goldberg 1986, 48)

Story starters are designed to elicit a form of writing that conforms to certain standards. Story starters are often used in large-scale evaluations of writing competence and get in the way of living twice through writing. They rarely allow students to write about topics they are interested in. Donald Graves (1976) calls the use of story starters "writing welfare" because students are dependent on their teachers for generic topics. Students rarely feel a sense of connection with the writing that stems from a story starter.

Teaching ideas in this chapter support students by allowing them to use their own lived experiences and knowledge as starting points for their writing. Students create idea banks or notebooks that act as "a wakeup call, a daily reminder to keep all [their] senses alert. This starts a cycle that reinforces itself. Writing down small details gets [students] in the habit of seeking out the important small things in [their] world. These details in turn often lead [them] to new material [they] never knew [they] had" (Fletcher 1996, 19). By engaging in the learning activities in this chapter, students begin to imagine the possibilities for their writing. They see that writing is an active process that involves more than sitting at a desk with writing tools. The following list of activities helps student writers generate ideas for their fiction writing.

Generating Ideas for Fiction Writing

1. Interview people you know and ask them about unusual, funny, or interesting things that have happened to them.
2. Observe people wherever you go. Ask yourself: What is unusual or interesting about these people? How could I use this to help me develop my character? (e.g., facial features, gestures, habits, clothing, what they say, how they act)
3. Read books, travel brochures, web sites, or visit a place that interests you. Try to use these resources to help develop a setting for your story.
4. List things that have happened to you that you will never forget.
5. Make lists of people and place names you might use in your stories.
6. Read stories and, at the same time, try to imagine how you or your story's characters would act in similar situations. If you could change the story and make it your own, what twists would you like the story to take?
7. Ask yourself, "What if…?"
8. Think about something surprising that happened to you recently.
9. Make a list of things that you wish would happen.

Alternatives to Story Starters

Mini-Lesson: Creating an Idea Bank, Personal Experiences

Students are able to write richer, more detailed, and more interesting stories when their stories are based on their own experiences. The process of creating an idea bank helps stir up memories of interesting personal experiences. A classroom where students tell stories about their lives helps student writers come up with ideas to create other stories and provides a motivation to write. The room buzzes with shared experiences, as students recognize that their lives are rich material for creating stories.

Goal for Student Writers

To generate topics for writing by reflecting on personal experiences.

Resources

Idea Bank template (Fig. 2.1)
Overhead Projection, "Maja's Idea Bank" (Fig. 2.2)
Chart, "Possible Categories for Ideas" (Fig. 2.3)
Students' idea banks (notebooks they use for generating and recording ideas)

Teacher and Students

The following quotes and examples from published children's authors show that authors draw on their own experiences when they write.

1. In the book, *Willow and Twig*, author Jean Little wrote about her own experiences with her niece and nephew as they bathed in a bathtub full of water and Metamucil. Read pages 181-182 to find out what happened. The children's blind uncle takes the role of Jean Little in the story.

2. Author Martyn Godfrey wanted to see how waves are created in a wave pool. He wrote about this personal experience in his version of an idea bank and saved it there until he decided he could use it in his book, *Meet you in the sewer*. Read pages 88-90 to find out what happened to Martyn as he tells the story of two children who relived his experience.

Some students will be eager to begin generating ideas using the idea bank template (Fig. 2.1); others will need examples. Use excerpts from Maja's Idea Bank (Fig. 2.2) to demonstrate to students how they can begin generating ideas to fill their own idea bank. The chart "Possible Categories for Ideas" (Fig. 2.3) can be used to spark students' thinking about unusual or interesting things that have happened in their lives, or to someone they know or have read about.

Students

This activity is most successful when students are encouraged to talk about the ideas they are putting in their idea bank. Students often come up with richer and more varied events and writing topics when they talk with peers about their ideas. Students can then refer to their idea banks whenever they are looking for ideas for writing. They should be encouraged to add to their idea banks throughout the year.

Children's Literature Used

Godfrey, M. 1993. *Meet you in the sewer*. Richmond Hill, ON: Scholastic.
Little, J. 2000. *Willow and Twig*. Toronto: Puffin Books.

_____'s Idea Bank

Category	Ideas

Fig. 2.1

GUIDED WRITING: STRATEGIES TO HELP STUDENTS BECOME BETTER WRITERS

Maja's Idea Bank

Category	Ideas
Sports	• Scoring winning goal and being named MVP for the hockey tournament • Spraining my ankle playing soccer
Pets/Animals	• Stray cat who fought our cat and ended up being our pet • Cat having kittens under my bed
Field trips	• Bus breaking down on the highway • Horse taking off without me
Family Vacation	• Going camping at the lake and bee stinging my sister on the lip when she was in the outhouse

Fig. 2.2

Possible Categories for ideas

daring things you've done

sports experiences

trying something new

family vacations

making/losing friends

something you've done that you feel proud of

strange or unusual happenings

embarrassing moments

field trips

outdoor adventures

buying something

losing/finding something

making/breaking something

painful moments

everyday school happenings

a first meeting

trips in cars, trains, subways, buses, airplanes

being with friends

pets/animals

humorous happenings

food experiences

disappointing moments

Fig. 2.3

Mini-Lesson: Creating an Idea Bank, Realistic and Historical Fiction

In this inductive lesson, students read several realistic or historical fiction books and identify common characteristics. They use a set of questions based on these characteristics to generate ideas for characters, problems, and settings for writing realistic or historical fiction.

Goal for Student Writers

To expand students' repertoires of writing ideas by recognizing and applying the characteristics of realistic or historical fiction (Fig. 2.4).

Resources

Realistic and historical fiction books (for examples, see page 25)
Chart, "Characteristics of Realistic and Historical Fiction" (Fig. 2.4)
Chart, "Generating Ideas for Writing Realistic and Historical Fiction" (Fig. 2.5)
Students' idea banks (Fig. 2.6)

Teacher and Students

Students become familiar with a number of books through listening to the teacher read, or by reading realistic or historical fiction. As a class, discuss what the stories have in common in terms of characters, setting, and problems.

Students

Students use the "Ideas for Writing Realistic and Historical Fiction" (Fig. 2.5) chart to generate character ideas, problems, and ideas for settings that they might use in their writing. Some students may not need these prompts. These students may even find that prompts get in the way of generating their own ideas. This activity is best used for those students who need support in generating ideas. Students might write stories or radio plays based on the ideas, or they might save the ideas for use in future realistic or historical fiction writing.

Characteristics of Realistic and Historical Fiction

The main characters act, talk, feel, and think in ways similar to the ways that people I know act, talk, feel, and think.

In historical fiction, the characters act in the same way people would have acted in the time period the story is set.

The stories take place in times and places that actually do exist, could exist, or, in the case of historical fiction, have existed.

The characters have problems that could happen to me and to people I know.

In historical fiction, the problems could have happened to people living in that time period.

Examples of realistic stories include mystery, adventure, humour, or stories about sports, animals, or school.

Fig. 2.4

Generating Ideas for Writing Realistic and Historical Fiction

Characters and Problems

1. What unusual habits could a character have?

   _____

2. What problem might the unusual habit cause?

   _____

3. What personality might a character have that would lead her/him to cause problems for other people or for themselves?

   _____

4. What problem might this personality trait cause for her/him?

   _____

5. What personality might a character have that would cause exciting, funny, or interesting things to happen? What exciting, funny, or interesting problem might this character have?

   _____

6. If you are writing historical fiction, what do you know about the lifestyles of the people in the place and time period that would create a problem for the character?

   _____

Settings

1. What kinds of homes might the characters have?

   _____

2. Who else lives with the different characters?

   _____

3. What could be unusual, funny, interesting, or dangerous about the setting?

   _____

4. If you are writing historical fiction, what do you know about lifestyles in the time period and place you want to write about?

   _____

Fig. 2.5

GATHERING IDEAS FOR WRITING

Ideas for Writing Realistic and Historical Fiction

Characters	Problems	Settings

Fig. 2.6

Realistic and Historical Fiction/Biography
(For teacher read-alouds and students' independent reading)

Realistic Fiction

Bloor, E. 1997. *Tangerine*. New York: Harcourt.

Cleary, B. 1999. *Ramona's world*. New York: HarperCollins.

Clements, A. 1996. *Frindle*. New York: Aladdin.

Creech, S. 1994. *Walk two moons*. London: Macmillan Books.

DiCamillo, K. 2000. *Because of Winn-Dixie*. Cambridge, MA: Candlewick.

Horvath, P. 2001. *Everything on a waffle*. Toronto: Groundwood Books.

Korman, G. 1998. *The sixth grade nickname game*. Markham, ON: Scholastic.

Little, J. 2000. *Willow and Twig*. Toronto: Puffin Books.

Park, B. 1995. *Mick Harte was here*. New York: Knopf.

Slipperjack, R. 2001. *Little voice*. Regina, SK: Coteau Books.

Historical Fiction/Biography

Beatty, P. 2000. *Lupita Mañana*. New York: Harper.

Curtis, C. P. 1999. *Bud, not Buddy*. New York: Dell Yearling.

Giff, P. R. 1997. *Lily's crossing*. New York: Dell Yearling.

Hest, A. 1997. *When Jessie came across the sea*. Cambridge, MA: Candlewick.

Hobbs, W. 1999. *Jason's gold*. New York: Harper.

Kamen, G. 1996. *Hidden music: The life of Fanny Mendelssohn*. New York: Atheneum.

Lottridge, C. 1997. *Wings to fly*. Toronto: Groundwood Books.

Lunn, J. 1997. *The hollow tree*. Toronto: Alfred Knopf.

McNaughton, J. 1996. *To dance at the Palais Royale*. Toronto: Stoddart.

Propp, V. W. 1999. *When the soldiers were gone*. New York: Putnam.

Mini-Lesson: Creating an Idea Bank, Fantasy

In this inductive lesson, students read a number of fantasy books and identify common characteristics. Students use a set of questions based on these characteristics to generate ideas for characters, problems, and settings for their own fantasy writing.

Goal for Student Writers

To expand students' repertoire of writing ideas by recognizing and applying the characteristics of fantasy.

Resources

Fantasy books (for examples, see page 30)
Chart, "Gathering Ideas for Writing Fantasy" (Fig. 2.7)
Chart, "Characteristics of Fantasy" (Fig. 2.8)
Students' idea banks (Fig. 2.9)

Teacher and Students

Through read-alouds by the teacher or through independent reading, students become familiar with a number of fantasy books. Students discuss what the stories have in common in terms of characters, setting, and problems.

Students

Students use the "Gathering Ideas for Writing Fantasy" (Fig. 2.7) chart to generate characters, problems, and settings that they might use in their own writing. Some students may not need these prompts and may find that the prompts get in the way of creatively generating their own ideas. This activity does not have to be compulsory for all students, only for those who need support in generating ideas.

Students might then write stories or plays mixing and blending these ideas, or they might save the ideas for use in future fantasy writing.

Gathering Ideas for Writing Fantasy

Use these questions to help think of characters, problems, and settings to write about.

Characters and Problems

1. What would you like to be able to do if you had magical or super-human powers? What would happen if you lost these powers?
   _____

2. How would a character with magical or superhuman powers cause problems for herself/himself or for others?
   _____

3. What unusual personality traits might an 'evil' character have? What problems might this 'evil' character create for a 'good' character?
   _____

4. What unusual personality traits might a 'good' character have? What problems might this 'good' character create for an 'evil' character?
   _____

5. What unusual personality might a talking animal or object have? What problems might this personality cause for the animal or object, and for others around him/her?
   _____

Settings

1. In a magical setting, what kinds of homes would the characters have?
   _____

2. What other kinds of living and nonliving things would be in this magical setting?
   _____

3. What would characters hear, see, smell, or touch in this magical setting?
   _____

© Portage and Main Press 2003. May be reproduced for classroom use. Note: photocopy at 121% for actual size

Fig. 2.7

GATHERING IDEAS FOR WRITING

Characteristics of Fantasy

The main characters have magical qualities that enable them to do things that I cannot do, yet the characteristics are believable.

Characters may also be animals that talk and have other human behaviours.

Fantasy stories take place in settings where magical things can happen.

The characters have problems where a 'good' force struggles with an 'evil' force, or the characters deal with magical or futuristic situations that disrupt otherwise normal lives.

Examples of fantasy stories:
stories about personified toys and objects
animal fantasy
fairy tales
time-slip fantasy
stories about extraordinary worlds
quest stories

Fig. 2.8

Ideas for Writing Fantasy

Characters	Problems	Settings

Fig. 2.9

GATHERING IDEAS FOR WRITING

© Portage and Main Press 2003. May be reproduced for classroom use. Note: photocopy at 121% for actual size

Fantasy
(For teacher read-alouds and students' independent reading)

Almond, D. 1998. *Skellig.* New York: Dell Yearling.

Cooper, S. 1993. *The boggart.* New York: Aladdin.

Farmer, N. 1994. *The ear, the eye and the arm.* New York: Puffin Books.

Goble, P. 1993. *The lost children.* New York: Simon & Schuster. (picture book)

Hunter, M. 1996. *The smartest man in Ireland.* San Diego: Magic Carpet Books.

Jacques, B. 2001. *Taggerung: A tale of Redwall.* London: Hutchison.

Oppel, K. 1997. *Silverwing.* Toronto: HarperCollins.

Pearson, K. 1996. *Awake and dreaming.* Toronto: Puffin Books.

Rowling, J. K. 1999. *Harry Potter and the chamber of secrets.* Vancouver: Raincoast Books.

Sachar, L. 1998. *Holes.* New York: Dell Yearling.

Scrimger, R. 1998. *The nose from Jupiter.* Toronto: Tundra Books.

NONFICTION

Teachers in grades four through seven confirm what researcher George Kamberelis (1999) says about primary students and nonfiction writing: students have less control of nonfiction forms of writing than they do of narrative forms. Why might this be? Is it because fiction writing comes more naturally to students? Perhaps fiction writing is more enjoyable for students? Or is it because they do not have a lot of experience writing nonfiction in earlier grades?

Christine Pappas (1993) argues that young children are able to communicate ideas in a non-narrative format orally, so they should be able to control a variety of written language genres as well. She says that narrative is not the only way that children are capable of representing their worlds in writing. Nor is narrative the genre that all students enjoy reading and writing about. David Booth (2002, 30) says, "many boys, including a large proportion of reluctant or limited readers, opt for nonfiction." Both girls and boys in elementary and middle-grade classrooms can become deeply engaged researching topics they find interesting. They need opportunities to do both fiction and nonfiction writing throughout the year.

Throughout this book, you will find ideas for supporting students' nonfiction writing—through creating idea banks for nonfiction writing, narrowing the focus for nonfiction writing, and searching for needed information on a topic. The goals are for students to develop their competence as nonfiction writers, and to see how they can use nonfiction writing to learn more about topics they are passionate and curious about. The following series of ideas is to help students create idea banks they can use specifically for nonfiction writing. Performing any one of the activities in the chart "Gathering Ideas for Nonfiction Writing" (Fig. 2.10) may help students gather ideas for nonfiction writing. In addition, teachers may use the two guided lessons in this chapter.

Gathering Ideas for Nonfiction Writing

1. List things that you think other people would like to know more about.
   _____
   _____

2. List things you have noticed recently that you want to know more about.
   _____
   _____

3. List things that you do well that you could show or teach other people.
   _____
   _____

4. List topics/ideas that you have read about lately that you would like to know more about.
   _____
   _____

5. List things that people have been talking about lately that you would like to know more about.
   _____
   _____

6. Talk with people you know about events, people, and issues that are in the news today. What questions come up? How could you find information to answer the questions?
   _____
   _____

7. List things that you use every day or most days (e.g., CD player, bicycle, tap water) that you would like to know more about. What questions do you have about how each thing works, or about how they came to be?
   _____
   _____

8. List things that are happening in your life, or in people's lives anywhere in the world, that you would like to see changed.
   _____
   _____

9. As you are reading any book of your choice, write the questions you have on sticky notes. Place the sticky notes in your idea bank.
   _____
   _____

Fig. 2.10

Mini-Lesson: Generating Topics to Achieve Many Purposes

Tony Stead (2002) believes that we have traditionally been too narrow in our use of nonfiction writing in classrooms. He urges us to look beyond report writing to include the multitude of nonfiction forms that we use in our everyday lives. In this mini-lesson, students examine the purposes of various types of nonfiction and identify topics they could use to achieve three purposes: **explaining, instructing,** and **persuading.**

Goal for Student Writers

To generate topics for nonfiction writing by thinking about what purpose the writing might serve.

Resources

Nonfiction that serves a number of purposes (suggestions on page 34)
Overhead Projection, "Matt's Nonfiction Idea Bank" (Fig. 2.11)
Nonfiction Idea Bank template (Fig. 2.12)

Teacher and Students

Using examples that explain, instruct, and persuade can show students that nonfiction writing is more than writing reports. The list provided below gives examples of nonfiction writing that are not in the report style. Teachers and students can discuss the topics and purposes of the nonfiction they read. Students can then think about topics they might want to write about. They can write in a persuasive manner, give instructions, or explain something. The excerpt from "Matt's Nonfiction Idea Bank" (Fig. 2.11) may help get students started in the nonfiction writing process. Some students will be eager to use the Nonfiction Idea Bank template (Fig. 2.12) to generate ideas; others will need further support and examples.

Students

Often, students come up with richer and more varied writing topics and events when they talk with peers about their ideas. Encourage students to refer to their idea banks whenever they are looking for writing ideas, and remind them to add to their idea banks throughout the year.

Nonfiction that Serves a Number of Purposes

Informing/Explaining

Questions/answers:

Berger, M., and Berger, G. 2000. *Can you hear a shout in space? Questions and answers about space exploration.* New York: Scholastic.

Wyatt, V. 2000. *Weather.* Toronto: Kids Can Press.

Catalogues:

Branzei, S. 2002. *Grossology.* New York: Penguin. (gross things are classified as slimy/mushy/oozy, crusty/scaly, or stinky/smelly)

Packard, M. 2001. *Ripley's believe it or not!* New York: Scholastic.

Letters/diaries:

Filipovic, Z. 1993. *Zlata's diary: A child's life in Sarajevo.* New York: Penguin.

UNICEF. (Ed.). 1994. *I dream of peace.* New York: HarperCollins.

Illustrations with captions:

Freedman, R. 1994. *Kids at work: Lewis Hine and the crusade against child labor.* New York: Clarion.

MacLeod, E. 2001. *Lucy Maud Montgomery: A writer's life.* Toronto: Kids Can Press.

Alphabet books:

Hunt, J. 1989. *Illuminations.* New York: Aladdin.

Major, K. 2000. *Eh? to zed.* Calgary, AB: Red Deer Press.

Instructing

Recipes/directions/experiments:

Iguchi, B. 1997. *The young snowboarder: A young enthusiast's guide to snowboarding.* Toronto: Stoddart.

Schwarz, R. 2002. *Making masks.* Toronto: Kids Can Press.

VanCleave, J. 1997. *Guide to the best science fair projects.* New York: John Wiley & Sons.

Wilkes, A. 2001. *Book of the seasons: Things to do all year round.* London: Usborne.

Persuading

Opinion letters/essays/advice to others:

Holyoke, N. 2001. *A smart girls' guide to boys: Surviving crushes, staying true to yourself and other stuff.* Middleton, WI: Pleasant Company Publications.

Roberts-Davis, T. 2001. *We need to go to school: Voices of the Rugmark children.* Toronto: Groundwood.

Advertisments:

Use ads from teen magazines that your students enjoy reading.

Matt's Nonfiction Idea Bank

Things I could explain to others	Things I could instruct others to do	Things I could persuade others to think/feel/do
Report on how Superman comics got started and where the ideas come from for making them	Directions on how to drive your teacher crazy	Advertisement for my favourite book
Alphabet book of hockey things	Map to get to all the arenas my hockey team plays in	Letter to my mom convincing her to let me go skiing with Kyle
Report on how the NHL started	Write up experiment for science class	Poster convincing my sister to stay out of my room

Fig. 2.11

Nonfiction Idea Bank

Things I could explain to others	Things I could instruct others to do	Things I could persuade others to think/feel/do

Fig. 2.12

© Portage and Main Press 2003. May be reproduced for classroom use. Note: photocopy at 121% for actual size

GATHERING IDEAS FOR WRITING

Mini-Lesson: Narrowing the Focus

Donald Graves (1989) says that when we begin teaching nonfiction writing we should place emphasis on subjects that are both interesting and have many sources of information that are readily available to students. Then, we should follow this up by supporting students in collecting information and giving the subject some focus. It is more important to help students organize a small amount of information toward a meaningful whole than to try to deal with large quantities of information that might be confusing to organize. With this in mind, the following mini-lesson invites students to ask questions about issues that are really important to them as they prepare to write an informational paper.

Goal for Student Writers
To use a webbing process to narrow a writing topic to a manageable size.

Resources
Nonfiction book of your choice
Topic web, "One Author's Decisions about the Topic" (Fig. 2.13)
Topic web template, "Narrowing the Topic" (Fig. 2.14)

Teacher and Students

It is worthwhile discussing problems that arise when writers choose topics with many possible directions. To start this discussion, question the choices made by the nonfiction writer of the chosen book. Question/answer books are useful for this discussion because they take on broad topics such as weather and outer space. The students and teacher might complete a web of various directions taken by the author after starting with the broad topic. An example (Fig. 2.13) for the book *Weather* is on page 39. Students might talk about other directions that the author could have taken, and they can speculate on why the writer chose not to take other directions.

Students

Students can look at their own topics and complete a web (Fig. 2.14) of various subtopics they might investigate while writing about their main topic. Students can then use various websites, print material, interviews, and other sources to determine which subtopics have a lot of information readily available to them, and which subtopics could be put together to form a coherent piece of writing. This is a useful exercise that helps narrow down the topic to a manageable size.

One Author's Decisions About the Topic
V. Wyatt, *Weather*

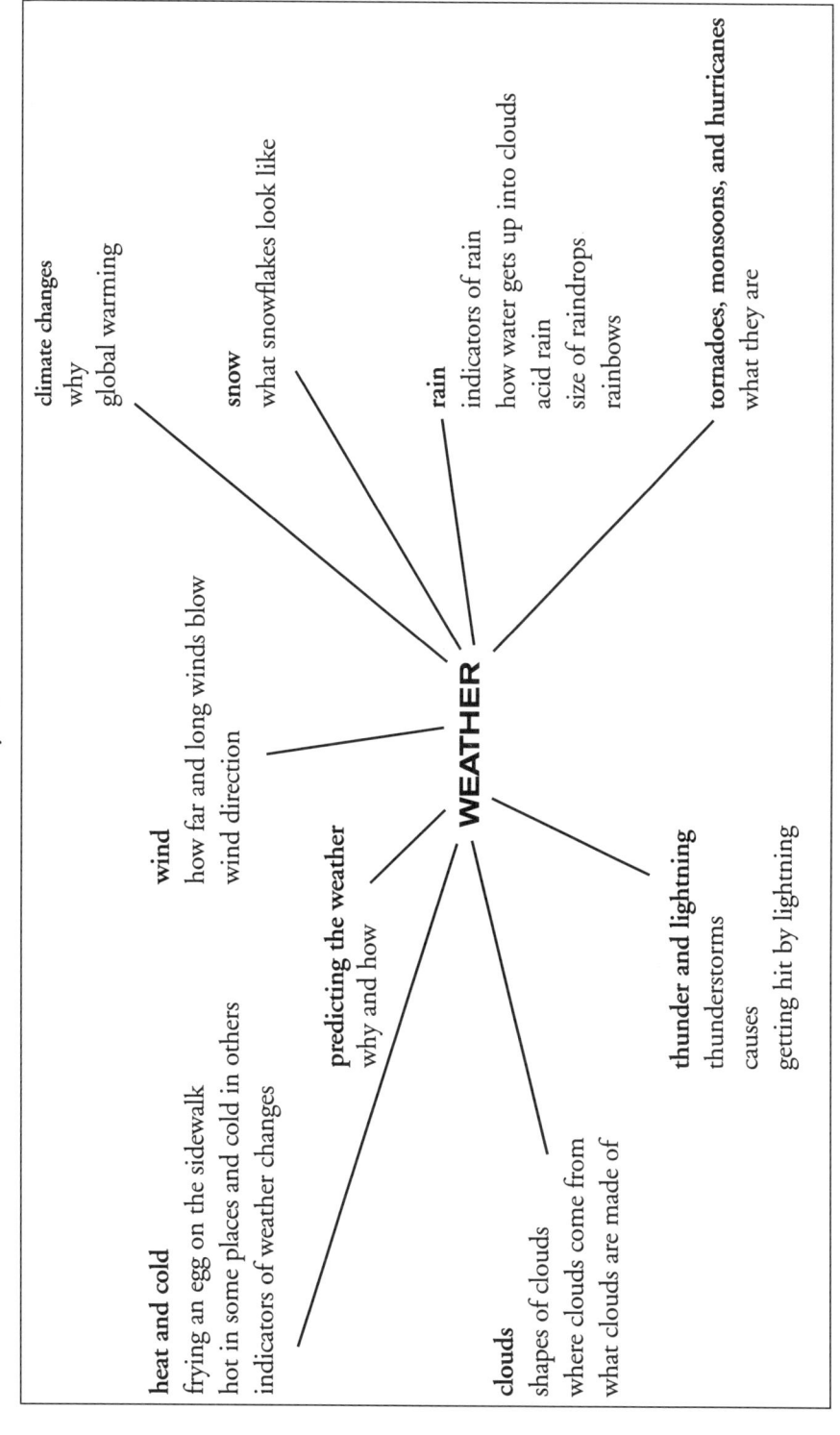

WEATHER

- climate changes
  - why
  - global warming

- snow
  - what snowflakes look like

- rain
  - indicators of rain
  - how water gets up into clouds
  - acid rain
  - size of raindrops
  - rainbows

- **tornadoes, monsoons, and hurricanes**
  - what they are

- **thunder and lightning**
  - thunderstorms
  - causes
  - getting hit by lightning

- **clouds**
  - shapes of clouds
  - where clouds come from
  - what clouds are made of

- **predicting the weather**
  - why and how

- **wind**
  - how far and long winds blow
  - wind direction

- **heat and cold**
  - frying an egg on the sidewalk
  - hot in some places and cold in others
  - indicators of weather changes

Fig. 2.13

© Portage and Main Press 2003. May be reproduced for classroom use. Note: photocopy at 121% for actual size

GATHERING IDEAS FOR WRITING

Narrowing the Topic

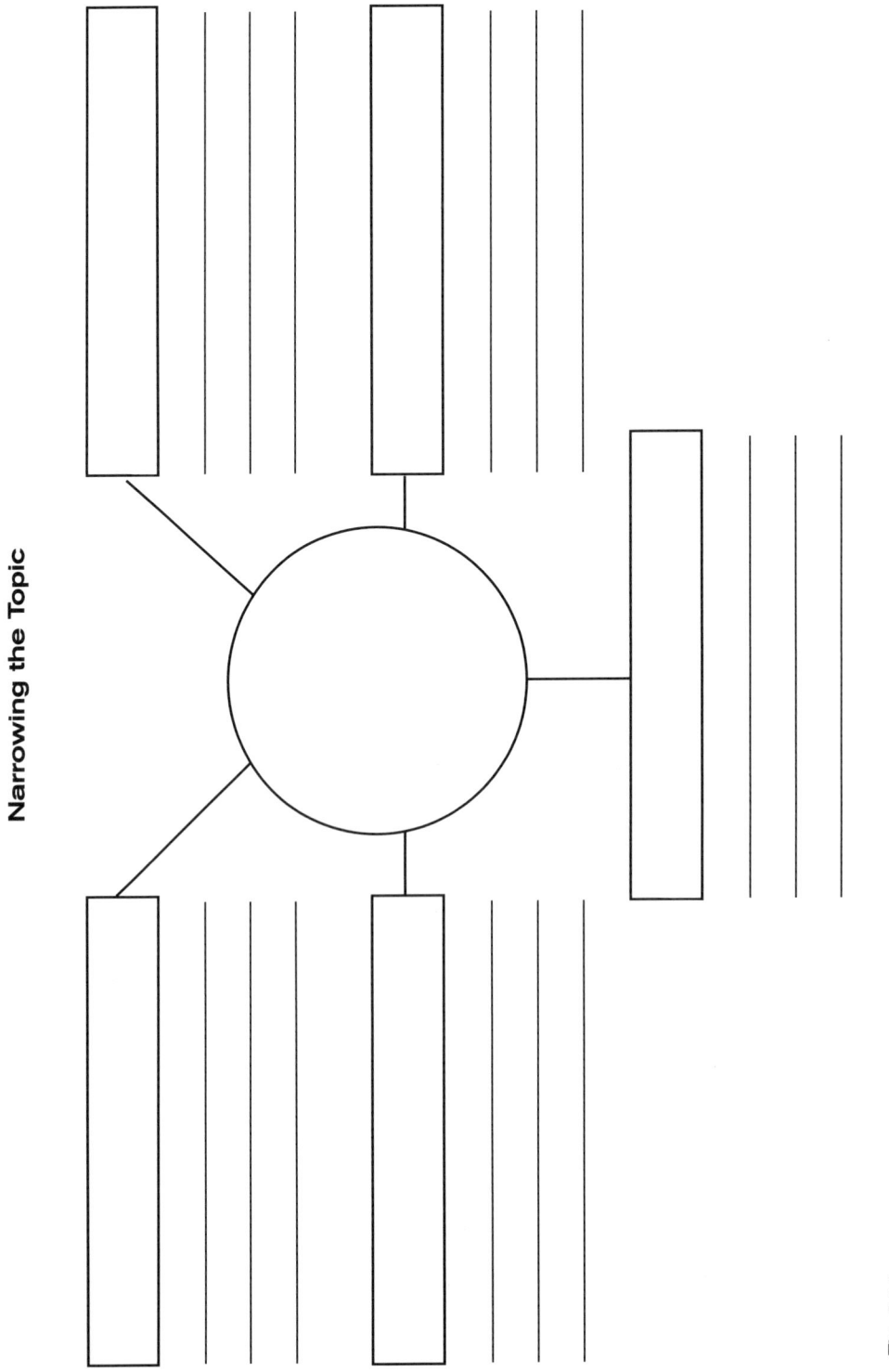

Fig. 2.14

REFERENCES

Booth, D. 2002. *Even hockey players read: Boys, literacy and learning.* Toronto: Pembroke Publishers.

Fletcher, R. 1996. *Breathing in breathing out: Keeping a writer's notebook.* Portsmouth, NH: Heinemann.

Goldberg, N. 1986. *Writing down the bones: Freeing the writer within.* Boston, MA: Shambhala.

Graves, D. 1976. Let's get rid of the welfare mess in the teaching of writing. *Language Arts*, 53, 645-651.

Graves, D. 1989. *Investigate nonfiction.* Portsmouth, NH: Heinemann.

Kamberelis, G. 1999. Genre development and learning: children writing stories, science reports, and poems. *Research in the Teaching of English*, 33(4), 403-460.

Pappas, C. C. 1993. Is narrative primary? Some insights from kindergartners' pretend readings of stories and information books. *Journal of Reading Behavior: A Journal of Literacy*, 25(1), 97-129.

Stead, T. 2002. *Is that a fact? Teaching nonfiction writing K-3.* Portland, ME: Stenhouse.

Wood Ray, K.. 1999. *Wondrous words: Writers and writing in the elementary classroom.* Urbana, IL: NCTE.

CHAPTER 3

Fiction—Character Development

CHARACTERS ARE INTEGRAL TO A GOOD STORY

Well-developed characters carry a story from its beginning to its satisfying end. Ralph Fletcher (1993, 56) writes: "character remains preeminent. The characters contain the crucial human link, that element of human destiny, for the reader to identify with." Characters are the most important part of a story. Their actions, thoughts, and words draw us into a story. Almost invariably, as we come to know our characters, the plot takes shape. We find that the characters show us where the story will go next.

Before moving to the mini-lessons on developing characters, it is important to consider gender stereotypes in classroom writing.

GENDER STEREOTYPES

Gender stereotyping comes up repeatedly in research on elementary and middle-grade students' writing (Gray-Schlegel and Gray-Schlegel 1995-96; Trepanier-Street and Romatowski 1991). According to these studies, boys have few female characters, and those they create are generally placed in positions of less power than the male characters. Male characters in boys' stories have powerful, risk-filled lives, and they are independent problem solvers. Girls, however, write their female characters in both powerful and powerless roles, and it is common to have male characters in the stories. Characters in girls' stories are more likely to resolve conflicts through creating relationships with others than through independent, aggressive action. Students are under great social pressures to write stories that have stereotypical female and male characters (Peterson 2001). Teachers need to create classroom settings where students feel comfortable writing about characters who act in untraditional feminine and masculine ways. Some helpful ways to achieve this type of classroom are:

- Voice questions and conflicts with gender expectations in response to student writing.
- Have conversations about the struggles that student writers might experience when writing about characters with non-stereotypical gender roles.

- Teach mini-lessons that involve skills for social change, such as supporting others who explore non-stereotypical gender meanings.
- Weave supportive feedback into the assessment process. Comment favourably on writing about characters who do not conform to stereotypes.

These strategies can broaden students' development of non-stereotypical characters in their writing. The mini-lessons in this chapter show students how to observe others in their world and note unique qualities the students might use to develop characters. The mini-lessons also show how students might adopt the strategies used by authors of children's and young adult literature. Indirectly, these mini-lessons may help students avoid using gender stereotypes when creating and developing characters in their narrative writing.

Mini-Lesson: Observing Others to Create Characters for Stories

Writers confide that they create characters by adding a pinch of someone they know (maybe even themselves) with a dash of many other people whom they have met throughout their lives. In an interview with Pamela Lloyd, Beverly Cleary (in Lloyd 1987, 75) says: "My characters come from both what I've seen and what I've imagined…My characters change and develop as I write." Steven Kellogg (in Lloyd 1987, 72) adds: "My characters come from inside me, usually. They also come from fragments of things and people, and experiences that I've had. I just use lots of different pieces of things that seem right and put them all together to create a character." These writers mix together the characteristics of many people to create characters who can do, say, and feel more than most real-life people can.

Goal for Student Writers

To learn about people and develop characters through observing people in their world, or in stories, movies, and television shows.

Resources

Student notebooks
Overhead projection/poster, "Things to Think About While Observing People" (Fig. 3.1)
Planning page, "Creating a Character from Observations" (Fig. 3.2)
Video of teacher's choice/preparations for a field trip to a bus/train station/ grocery store/other places in the community where many people congregate

Teacher and Students

The poster, "Things to Think About While Observing People" (Fig. 3.1) can help guide students' observations of people in a video or in the world outside the school. Students do not have to restrict their observations to these situations. The students can share their observations in small groups upon returning to the classroom or after viewing clips of the video. They can discuss how particular characteristics might be blended to form characters for their stories, or how characters they have already created might develop through incorporating some of the characteristics of people they have observed.

Students

Students develop characters by pulling together characteristics of the people they find interesting and suitable to their story. Students can use characteristics of a number of people they think would work well in their writing or characteristics of one person who stood out to them as someone they might write about.

Things to Think About While Observing People

What is interesting or unusual about the person you are observing?

- **facial features and/or facial expressions**

- **clothing**

- **gestures or posture**

- **voice, or the things he or she says**

- **relationships with others**

© Portage and Main Press 2003. May be reproduced for classroom use. Note: photocopy at 121% for actual size

Fig. 3.1

Planning Page

Creating a Character from Observations

1. What does your character look like? What kind of clothing does your character wear?
   _____
   _____
   _____

2. What is your character's name?
   _____
   _____
   _____

3. What does this character do that stands out from others?
   _____
   _____
   _____

4. What kinds of problems could your character have? In what interesting situations could your character find himself/herself?
   _____
   _____
   _____

5. Who might help the character with his/her problems? What qualities does this other character have to help solve problems?
   _____
   _____
   _____

6. How does this character treat other people?
   _____
   _____
   _____

Fig. 3.2

FICTION—CHARACTER DEVELOPMENT

© Portage and Main Press 2003. May be reproduced for classroom use. Note: photocopy at 121% for actual size

Mini-Lesson: Character Development

Students may develop characters through physical description, actions, words, and others' thoughts about the character.

Goal for Student Writers

To develop characters using a combination of any or all of the following:

- physical description of the character
- actions of the character
- others' thoughts about the character

Resources

Overhead projection, "Character Development: Learning from Other Writers" (Fig. 3.3)

Fiction of the teacher's choice, or choose examples from "Books Providing Models for Character Development" (page 50)

Teacher and Students

Before reading, the teacher asks students to think about words that describe the character who is the focus of the passage. Students should think about what words and phrases the author uses to give the character specific traits. What words created the impression of the character? Read the character description, and ask students:

1. "What kind of a person is _____?"
2. Does the writer ever describe the personality directly?
3. If not, what does the writer do to show us that _____ is this kind of person?

The students' responses may be recorded on the overhead projection, "Character Development: Learning from Other Writers" (Fig. 3.3).

Students

Students can use a combination of techniques learned in the mini-lessons to create character descriptions for stories they are currently writing. They may also create new characters for stories they plan to write in the future.

Students may opt to write a speech about a character while imagining that they are honouring (or perhaps roasting) the character at a banquet.

Character Development: Learning from Other Writers

Character's Personality	What the writer does to show what the character is like

Fig. 3.3

FICTION—CHARACTER DEVELOPMENT

Books Providing Models for Character Development

Cleary, B. 1999. *Ramona's world.* New York: HarperCollins.

Daisy's mom is introduced on pages 46-48 through a physical description, her words and actions, and Ramona's thoughts about her.

Clements, A. 1996. *Frindle.* New York: Aladdin.

Mrs. Granger is introduced through her actions, physical description, and her reputation on pages 6-11.

Horvath, P. 2001. *Everything on a waffle.* Toronto: Groundwood Books.

On pages 29-33 readers come to know Miss Honeycut through a physical description, her actions, her words, and the ways that others react to her and think about her.

Naylor, P. R. 1991. *Shiloh.* New York: Dell.

On pages 22-24 Judd Travers is introduced through his actions, words, and Marty's thoughts about him.

Oppel, K. 1997. *Silverwing.* Toronto: HarperCollins.

Marina is introduced through physical description, her speech, and Shade's thoughts about her on pages 67-70.

Rowling, J. K. 1997. *Harry Potter and the philosopher's stone.* Vancouver: Raincoast Books.

On pages 79-80 Hermione is introduced through her actions and words, her physical description, and other characters' reactions to and thoughts about her.

Mini-Lesson: Developing Characters Using Dialogue

Readers come to know characters in stories through their dialogue in much the same way we come to know people through what they say. The trick for writers is to use dialogue in appropriate places that fit with their actions and motivations. Information is also needed in the dialogue to keep the plot moving. Often upper-elementary and middle-grade students use dialogue that slows down the story line. It does not go beyond basic "hello, how are you" exchanges. While these are certainly part of real-life conversations, they do not make for riveting reading. In this lesson, students assess what published authors do to create natural dialogue that helps develop characters and plot. Students can then incorporate what they have learned into their own writing.

Goal for Student Writers

To use dialogue to enhance character development and plot.

Resources

Fiction of teacher's choice or choose from examples provided in "Books Providing Models for Dialogue" (below)
Overhead projection, "Dialogue: Learning from Other Writers" (Fig. 3.4)

Teacher and Students

Students act out roles of characters as they read passages from selected books. The books have dialogue that is particularly strong in developing characters and plot. Students then identify the kinds of information that the dialogue provides. What makes the dialogue seem natural for the characters? In what parts of the story does the writer use dialogue? The students' responses may be recorded on the overhead projection, "Dialogue: Learning from Other Writers" (Fig. 3.4).

Students

Students identify places in their stories where dialogue might be used. They write dialogue using a combination of techniques learned in the mini-lesson.

Books Providing Models for Dialogue

Curtis, C. P. 1999. *Bud, not Buddy.* New York: Yearling.
> Readers experience the first meeting of Bud and his grandfather through the conversation between the two characters on pages 146-152.

DiCamillo, K. 2000. *Because of Winn-Dixie.* Cambridge, MA: Candlewick Press.

The conversation between Opal and her father about whether Winn-Dixie, the Less Fortunate dog, can stay with them, takes place on pages 16-19.

Ellis, D. 2000. *The breadwinner.* Toronto: Groundwood.

The family's discussion around a trip to Mazar-e-Sharif for Nooria to get married takes place on pages 135-137.

Little, J. 2000. *Willow and Twig.* Toronto: Puffin.

Willow and her grandmother talk about Twig going to a school with other deaf and hard-of-hearing children on pages 203-204.

Oppel, K. 1997. *Silverwing.* Toronto: HarperCollins.

In the first chapter, Chinook's personality and the influence he has over other young bats in the colony are conveyed through dialogue between Chinook, Shade, and other bats. The dialogue also carries forward the event that brought the owls' wrath on the colony.

Walter, E. 1997. *Trapped in ice.* Toronto: Penguin.

On pages 9-12, readers experience Mrs. Kiruk's first meeting with the Captain through the angry dialogue between the two characters.

Dialogue: Learning from Other Writers

At what points in the story does the author use dialogue?	What does the author do to make the dialogue seem natural for the characters?	What kinds of information do you learn from the dialogue?

Fig. 3.4

FICTION—CHARACTER DEVELOPMENT

REFERENCES

Fletcher, R. 1993. *What a writer needs.* Portsmouth, NH: Heinemann.

Gray-Schlegel, M., & Gray-Schlegel, T. 1995-96. An investigation of gender stereotypes as revealed through children's creative writing. *Reading Research and Instruction,* 35, 160-170.

Lloyd, P. 1987. *How writers write.* Melbourne, AU: Methuen Australia Pty. Ltd.

Peterson, S. 2001. Gender identities and self-expression in classroom narrative writing. *Language Arts,* 78(5), 451-457.

Trepanier-Street, M., & Romatowski, J. A. 1991. Achieving sex equity goals: Implications from creative writing research. *Educational Horizons,* 70(1), 34-40.

CHAPTER 4

Developing and Organizing Ideas

FICTION

Many teachers try to support students in their writing by giving plot structure frameworks to help identify what was happening at the beginning, middle, and end of their stories. Often, when students use these frameworks their writing ends up being a string of events that do not have a sense of story. It seems that students simply rewrite the events from the planning page rather than use their plans as a starting point for fleshing out a story.

Published authors help students and teachers resolve this problem. Many authors (but not all) say that they start their stories by getting to know their characters first (Lloyd 1987). When authors know their characters well, they find that their characters lead the story through the initiating events, rising action, and climax of the stories. In many cases, the authors are surprised about the twists and turns that their story lines take, and would not have thought of such actions and events in their initial planning.

Charting out events in the stories is worthwhile for some students. However, it is very likely that students' stories will not go exactly as planned. They should expect surprises as their characters move through their adventures toward the ending. In this chapter, there are mini-lessons on writing leads and helping students think about possible paths for their stories.

Different Ways of Telling Stories

Different cultures value different ways of telling stories. Sarah Michaels (1981) and Shirley Brice Heath (1983) looked at the different narrative styles of children from culturally distinct communities. They found that teachers responded more favourably to children who used narrative styles similar to those of European storytelling styles—with a beginning, middle, and end, and all the ideas related to one topic. Many African American and Aboriginal children told and wrote stories that were more loosely connected chains of actions or events. The children did not usually state the topic directly in their narratives. David Bloome (1991) says that it is important for teachers to be aware of cultural differences in organizing ideas and events within stories. If teachers understand this they can better appreciate what each student brings to the classroom, and they can learn new storytelling styles in the process. Teachers can also become more effective in broadening students' repertoires of storytelling styles. The following rubric takes different storytelling styles into account.

Mini-Lesson: Creating Captivating Leads Using Different Approaches

There are as many approaches to introducing a story as there are authors. Often, because getting started is one of the hardest parts of writing a story, formulating ideas to introduce stories is helpful to students. In this mini-lesson, published writers help guide students toward creating interesting leads through the use of a number of different approaches.

Goal for Student Writers

To use various approaches to writing leads based on leads used by published authors of children's literature.

Resources

Examples of leads from published literature
Chart, "Possibilities for Creating Leads" (Fig. 4.1)

Teacher and Students

Read the leads from selected stories on the list "Possibilities for Creating Leads" (Fig. 4.1), or from other books, and discuss with students how they can use such approaches in writing leads for their own stories. Use the analytic rubric (Fig. 4.2) to help assess students' choices of leads.

Students

Students revise the lead to one of their stories, or they create a new lead using what they have learned from published authors and read them to a partner. They should ask the partner to identify which approach the student writer has taken and give feedback on how the writer might use the approach even more effectively.

Possibilities for Creating Leads

Describe the character's ordinary life and what happened to change her/his life.

Example: The day Shiloh come, we're having us a big Sunday dinner. Dara Lynn's dipping bread in her glass of cold tea, the way she likes, and Becky pushes her beans up over the edge of her plate in her rush to get 'em down. Ma gives us her scolding look. "Just once in my life," she says, "I'd like to see a bite of food go direct from the dish into somebody's mouth without a detour of any kind." She's looking at me when she says it, though. It isn't that I don't like fried rabbit. Like it fine. I just don't want to bite down on buckshot, is all, and I'm checking each piece (*Shiloh* 1991, 11).

Describe the sights, smells, and sounds of the setting.

Example: When animal droppings and garbage and spoiled straw are piled up in a great heap, the rotting and moiling give forth heat. Usually no one gets close enough to notice because of the stench. But the girl noticed and, on that frosty night, burrowed deep into the warm, rotting muck, heedless of the smell. In any event, the dung heap probably smelled little worse than everything else in her life—the food scraps scavenged from kitchen yards, the stables and sties she slept in when she could, and her own unwashed, unnourished, unloved, and unlovely body (*The Midwife's Apprentice* 1995, 1).

Foreshadow an event that will happen in the story.

Example: I stood there, looking around, and that's when I saw the face pressed up against an upstairs window next door. It was a round girl's face, and it looked afraid. I didn't know it then, but that face belonged to Phoebe Winterbottom, a girl who had a powerful imagination, who would become my friend, and who would have many peculiar things happen to her (*Walk Two Moons* 1994, 2).

Introduce the characters through how they usually behave toward one another.

Example: My father beat my mother with his belt. And when I tried to grab him one time, stop him, he beat me with the belt, too. Now he was beating both of us all the time. When he beat my mother he would beat her with the buckle end of the belt. But when he beat me he would turn the belt around and hold the other end so that he'd be beating me with the end that didn't have the buckle on. My mother told me that he did that because he liked me better (*Uncle Ronald* 1996, 8).

Fig. 4.1

Draw in the reader with a question and the character's thoughts about her/his situation.

Example: Don't you hate it when everyone in the room is wearing clothes and you're not? The doctor's wearing a dress with a white coat on top, and the nurse has on one of those green uniforms. Mom's wearing her new tweed suit—a bit wrinkled after a day at work and half the night sitting beside my bed—but still, a suit. And me? I have underpants. Period. I had a hospital gown that didn't do up the right way, but they made me take it off. So now I'm wearing dark green Y-fronts and a smile, and that's about it. No, I forgot. I have a bandage on. It isn't doing me much good, modesty-wise, because it's on my head (*The Nose from Jupiter* 1998, 1).

Introduce the characters through dialogue.

Example: "I'll race you to the corner, Ellen!" Annemarie adjusted the thick leather pack on her back so that her schoolbooks balanced evenly. "Ready?" She looked at her best friend. Ellen made a face. "No," she said, laughing. "You know I can't beat you—my legs aren't as long. Can't we just walk, like civilized people?" She was a stocky ten-year-old, unlike lanky Annemarie. "We have to practice for the athletic meet on Friday—I know I'm going to win the girls' race this week. I was second last week, but I've been practicing every day. Come on, Ellen," Annemarie pleaded, eyeing the distance to the next corner of the Copenhagen street. "Please?" (*Number the Stars* 1989, 1).

Fig. 4.1 (cont'd)

Analytic Rubric for Narrative Writing • Considering Multiple Storytelling Styles

	Below grade-level expectations	Approaching grade-level expectations	Meets grade-level expectations	Exceeds grade-level expectations
Content and Organization	Provides general ideas with no supporting details	Provides a few specific supporting details	Provides some specific supporting details	Provides specific supporting details consistently
	Makes little or no attempt to engage readers	Makes some attempt to engage readers	Includes information designed to create some emotional reaction from readers	Includes information designed to create strong emotional reactions from readers
	Does not use enough events/actions/ideas to discern an organizational structure	Unevenly uses the chosen organizational structure	Uses the chosen organizational structure fairly consistently	Consistently uses the chosen organizational structure
	Recycles tried-and-true ideas	Shows a weak attempt to experiment with new ideas/structures, and so on	Experiments with new ideas/structures to some degree	Experiments with new ideas/structures, and so on in an engaging way
Vocabulary	Uses limited vocabulary and may use language inappropriately	Uses general words and expressions	Uses some specific words and expressions	Uses specific words and expressions in a lively and effective way
Sentence Structure	Uses simple sentences only	Sometimes uses simple and compound sentences correctly	Uses simple and compound sentences correctly and sometimes uses complex sentences	Uses simple, compound, and complex sentences correctly
Conventions	Consistently makes spelling, grammar, and punctuation errors that interfere with communication	Sometimes makes spelling, grammar, and punctuation errors that interfere with communication	Generally uses correct spelling, grammar, and punctuation	Consistently uses correct spelling, grammar, and punctuation

Fig. 4.2

Leads from Published Literature

Creech, S. 1994. *Walk two moons.* London: Macmillan.

Cushman, K. 1995. *The midwife's apprentice.* New York: HarperCollins.

Doyle, B. 1996. *Uncle Ronald.* Toronto: Groundwood.

Lowry, L. 1989. *Number the stars.* New York: Dell Yearling.

Naylor, P. R. 1991. *Shiloh.* New York: Dell Yearling.

Scrimger, R. 1998. *The nose from Jupiter.* Toronto: Tundra.

Mini-Lesson: Generating Possible Story Lines

In this mini-lesson, students generate possible story lines, problems, and events that follow from the introduction and lead to the problem situations.

Goal for Student Writers

To write stories with plots that move toward a satisfying ending by using a strategy to generate possible events and actions.

Resources

Template, "Paths Characters Might Follow" (Fig. 4.3)
Leads from stories selected by the teacher

Teacher and Students

The template, "Paths Characters Might Follow" (Fig. 4.3), serves as the starting point for the lesson. Students and their teacher consider the personalities of characters from a lead that the teacher has written, or a lead from one of the stories used in the previous mini-lesson. The students generate problems the characters might encounter, and then brainstorm to come up with as many different ways as possible for the characters to get into the problem situations and then resolve them. Students might consider the following:

- What is the character's main goal?
- What and/or who could get in the way of achieving that goal?
- What personality changes might be good for the character?
- What are logical consequences of the character's actions?
- What and/or who could help the character achieve the goal?
- What special qualities does the character have that might help her/him achieve the goal?

Students

Students determine possible problem situations for the characters they have developed. They then think about how the characters might get into the problem situations and what the characters could do to resolve the problems, generating as many possibilities as they can think of. They write with the recognition that their characters may take detours and end up at in entirely unanticipated places or situations.

Paths Characters Might Follow

Problem situations	Ways to get into the problem situation	Ways to get out of the problem situations

Fig. 4.3

GUIDED WRITING: STRATEGIES TO HELP STUDENTS BECOME BETTER WRITERS

Nonfiction

Marilyn Chapman (1997, 211) tells us that "form follows function." She explains that writers determine what they want to achieve in a particular context and accordingly choose the appropriate form of writing. When writers follow the expected (conventional) organizational framework of a particular form (e.g., an opinion letter), readers can readily make sense of the text and use it for their own purposes. Students learn the various forms of writing when they have a true-to-life context for their writing. They develop their knowledge of the purposes of nonfiction writing and the organizational frameworks for each form. They can do this through reading and creating their own persuasive letters, biographies, informational essays, advertisement brochures, or other nonfiction forms of writing. Learning different nonfiction forms for representing ideas and thoughts provides greater choice when students are writing in a workshop setting.

Researchers Freedman and Medway (1994) say that genres or forms of writing used by writers of all ages have no fixed formats. Instead, they are social actions that are derived from and related "to the writer's social motive in responding to a recurrent social situation of a certain type" (3). We may teach students the features of a particular form of writing (biography, for example), but we also show how the form is different depending on the topic, the author's purpose, intended audience, time, and place in which the author wrote, and so on. The emphasis in teaching and assessing nonfiction writing should be based on the student's ability to communicate ideas in order to achieve their intended purpose, not on following a particular format precisely.

The mini-lessons that follow present possibilities for students to write leads and organize their ideas for nonfiction writing.

Mini-Lesson: Writing Effective Leads

As with writing fiction, the leads of nonfiction writing should draw readers into the writing and provide sufficient information to give readers a sense of what the writing is about. In this mini-lesson, students analyze published literature to determine approaches they can take when writing leads for their nonfiction writing.

Goal for Student Writers

To write an effective lead for a nonfiction piece of writing through experimentation with different types of leads.

Resources

Various nonfiction texts
Chart, "Possibilities for Creating Leads: Nonfiction" (Fig. 4.4)
Chart, "What Do Authors Do?" (Fig. 4.5)

Teacher and Students

After reading leads from the list provided in "Possibilities for Creating Leads: Nonfiction" (Fig. 4.4), students and their teacher discuss which types of leads work best for achieving the writers' purposes. They can then complete the chart, "What Do Authors Do?" (Fig. 4.5) and consider the words, phrases, and types of information that the author provides.

Students

Students talk with a partner about the types of leads that might work best for the pieces they are working on. They experiment with that type of lead or revise the lead they have already written so that it provides sufficient information and is presented in a way that will capture the reader's interest.

Possibilities for Creating Leads: Nonfiction

1. Ask a question that invites readers into the writing.

   How do you tell a friend that you're excited? Do you shout? Do you open your eyes wide? Do you jump up and down? If you do any of these things, you are communicating with your friend. (*Animal Talk*, 4)

2. Use a quotation to give additional authority to the writing.

   "I will tell you today, dear Fanny, that in all essential points, all that is important, I am so much satisfied with you that I have no wish left." Abraham Mendelssohn, November 1828 (*Hidden Music,* 1)

3. Tell an anecdote that shows what the writing is all about.

   I first heard of Zlata Filipovié in the summer of 1993 when a Bosnian friend told me about a young girl who was being called "the Anne Frank of Sarajevo." I found out that Zlata was a thirteen-year-old girl, living with her parents, who had been keeping a diary since September 1991, a few months before the first barricades went up in the city and the heavy shelling began. (*Zlata's Diary*, v)

4. Provide background information so readers understand the importance of the writing.

   You can see so many different things around you. You use your eyes to see a tiny insect, or a star billions of miles away, or a rocket thundering off a launch pad. Yet all around you are countless sights that your eyes cannot see. There are worlds that are too small, too distant, too fast. There are worlds that are behind or within other objects. And there are kinds of light that your eyes just cannot see. . . This book explores some of the worlds around you that your eyes cannot see. (*Out of Sight,* Introduction)

Fig. 4.4

5. Introduce points of view that might be taken while reading.

   To us, today, the race seems peculiar. It consisted of two fit young men running around the small track at Madison Square Garden in New York City 262 times. This event took place on the night of December 15, 1908, and it involved the two competitors circling the track time after time to cover the marathon distance of 26 miles, 385 yards (42.2 kilometres). . . .But in the early years of the 20th century, such events as the Tom Longboat-Dorando Pietri race were all the rage. Fourteen thousand roaring spectators packed the Garden to cheer the runners that night, and hundreds more—unable to buy a ticket for the sold-out event—milled in the streets outside, impatient to learn the race's outcome. (*The Man who Ran Faster than Everyone*, 1)

6. Explain what the writing is all about.

   Hana's suitcase is a true story that takes place on three continents over a period of almost seventy years. It brings together the experiences of a girl and her family in Czechoslovakia in the 1930s and 40s, a young woman and a group of children in Tokyo, Japan, and a man in Toronto, Canada, in modern times. (*Hana's Suitcase*, v)

7. Show readers how they can use the writing.

   Masks are fun! They have been used for celebrations and ceremonies, dances and plays for thousands of years. . . For parties, plays or dressing up, masks are great! Hidden behind a mask, you can become anyone or anything. So, for serious acting or simply for silly fun, make a mask. (*Making Masks*, 4)

Fig. 4.4 (cont'd)

What Do Authors Do?

Title	Words and Phrases that Capture Your Interest	Kinds of Information Provided

Fig. 4.5

DEVELOPING AND ORGANIZING IDEAS

© Portage and Main Press 2003. May be reproduced for classroom use. Note: photocopy at 121% for actual size

Nonfiction

Batten, J. 2002. *The man who ran faster than everyone: The story of Tom Longboat.* Toronto: Tundra.

Filipovi, Z. 1993. *Zlata's diary: A child's life in Sarajevo.* London: Viking.

Kamen, G. 1996. *Hidden music: The life of Fanny Mendelssohn.* New York: Atheneum.

Kaner, E. 2002. *Animal talk: How animals communicate through sight, sound and smell.* Toronto: Kids Can Press.

Levine, K. 2002. *Hana's suitcase.* Toronto: Second Story Press.

Schwarz, R. 2002. *Making masks.* Toronto: Kids Can Press.

Simon, S. 2000. *Out of sight: Pictures of hidden worlds.* New York: SeaStar Books.

Mini-Lesson: Organizing Ideas and Using Headings

Next to finding a manageable topic, organizing the information that students gather is probably the hardest part of nonfiction writing. An effective process is to look for headings that describe pieces of information that seem to fit together. The following mini-lesson guides students through this process.

Goal for Student Writers

To use headings to organize nonfiction writing.

Resources

Overhead projection, "Data Sample" (Fig. 4.6)
Chart, "Organizing the Data" (Fig. 4.7)

Teacher and Students

The teacher and students read through the information in the "Data Sample" (Fig. 4.6) and identify bits of information that could be put together in one category. Someone cuts up the overhead projection so that these pieces can be placed together. Students and their teacher then think of headings that describe what the pieces of information have in common. They continue this process until all the information has been categorized, and then discuss an appropriate order for the information to be placed. The overhead transparency, "Organizing the Data" (Fig. 4.7) can be used to record their decisions.

Students

Students can work on the data they have gathered in the same way they worked with the teacher. It is best if the students have used only one side of the page to write their notes. This way they can cut the notes out and place bits of information together into appropriate categories.

Students use the headings they have generated to organize the information to write their nonfiction.

Data Sample

Tobacco products contain nicotine. Nicotine is addictive and poisonous.

Smoking causes heart disease and lung, larynx, oral, esophagus, bladder, and pancreas cancer.

Carbon monoxide is emitted (400 times greater than what is considered safe in industrial settings). Carbon monoxide interferes with ability of blood to transport oxygen inside the body.

Sidestream smoke comes from burning cigarettes between puffs. It has more nicotine and carcinogenic things in it than smoke inhaled by smokers.

When smokers quit, their risk of developing diseases and conditions drops to nonsmokers' risks after a few years.

Laws should restrict sponsorship of events and access to tobacco products by minors.

There should be restrictions on advertising, promotion, and product display in stores.

Labels on packages should send strong messages about the dangers of smoking.

Governments should regulate what can go into cigarettes and what can be emitted from them.

Fig. 4.6

Organizing the Data

Instructions

Using the notes you have made about your topic, pile the notes with common topics in one stack. Write headings that describe what all the notes in each pile have in common. You could also use labelled envelopes to keep all the notes together.

Note: You may need more than one page to organize all your data.

Heading _____

Notes: _____

_____

_____

_____

Heading _____

Notes: _____

_____

_____

_____

Heading _____

Notes: _____

_____

_____

_____

Fig. 4.7

DEVELOPING AND ORGANIZING IDEAS

© Portage and Main Press 2003. May be reproduced for classroom use. Note: photocopy at 121% for actual size

Mini-Lesson: Writing Using Paragraphs

Simply knowing the structure of a paragraph is not enough when organizing information into paragraphs. Students should use paragraphs to show how ideas and information fit together in nonfiction writing. This lesson is intended to help students develop this skill.

Goal for Student Writers

To use paragraphs to organize nonfiction writing.

Resources

"Persuasive Essay, version 1" (Fig. 4.8)
"Persuasive Essay, version 2" (Fig. 4.9)

Teacher and Students

Students read through the persuasive essays, thinking about which one is easier to read, and why. The teacher explains that writers can group ideas and information that belong together in paragraphs. The students and their teacher read through Persuasive Essay, version 1, (Fig. 4.8) and circle the ideas that seem to go together. They then write key words or phrases beside the circled ideas. These summarize what the key words have in common. These key words are the topics of paragraphs that could better organize the writing.

Students and teacher compare and contrast the sentences they grouped together with the paragraphs that the writer created in Persuasive Essay, version 2 (Fig. 4.9) of the essay. They identify the key ideas within each of the paragraphs in version 2 and compare and contrast them with the key ideas they identified in their groupings of sentences in version 1.

Students

Students read their own nonfiction writing and circle the ideas that go together. These common ideas could form one paragraph. Students then write a key word or phrase that captures the central idea of each paragraph in their writing. They then revise their writing, using paragraphs to show which ideas go together.

Persuasive Essay • Version 1

Media Influences on Girls

Girls have a lot of pressure to look like the girls in teen zines. I think girls in grade 5 shouldn't have to worry about looking like those magazine ad girls. We all are cute in our own way. When I look at the zines I see girls who are skinny and look like they never have to go on a diet. They are skinny without even trying. They always look so happy in the pictures. When I look at my friends, I see some girls who are skinny and some who are medium-sized and some who are bigger. My friends talk about being on diets sometimes. Lots of my friends wish they could look like the magazine girls. I want to tell them that I think they look good just like they are. Who cares if they have to pop zits every other day and they don't have designer clothes? So I say to my friends in grade 5 that we should not worry about having perfect figures and cute faces like magazine girls. I think we're all pretty just the way we are.

Fig. 4.8

Persuasive Essay • Version 2

Media Influences on Girls

Girls have a lot of pressure to look like the girls in teen zines. I think girls in grade 5 shouldn't have to worry about looking like those magazine ad girls. We all are cute in our own way.

When I look at the zines I see girls who are skinny and look like they never have to go on a diet. They are skinny without even trying. They always look so happy in the pictures.

When I look at my friends, I see some girls who are skinny and some who are medium-sized and some who are bigger. My friends talk about being on diets sometimes. Lots of my friends wish they could look like the magazine girls. I want to tell them that I think they look good just like they are. Who cares if they have to pop zits every other day and they don't have designer clothes? So I say to my friends in grade 5 that we should not worry about having perfect figures and cute faces like magazine girls. I think we're all pretty just the way we are.

Fig. 4.9

REFERENCES

Bloome, D. 1991. Anthropology and research on teaching the English language arts. In J. Flood, J.M. Jensen, D. Lapp, and J.R. Squire (eds.), *Handbook of research on teaching the English language arts* (pp. 46-56). New York: Macmillan.

Chapman, M. 1997. *Weaving webs of meaning: Writing in the elementary school.* Toronto: ITP Nelson.

Freedman, A., & Medway, P. 1994. Introduction: New views of genre and their implications for education. In A. Freedman & P. Medway (Eds.), *Learning and teaching genre* (pp. 1-22). Portsmouth, NH: Heinemann.

Heath, S. B. 1983. *Ways with words: Language, life, and work in communities and classrooms.* Cambridge: Cambridge University Press.

Lloyd, P. 1987. *How writers write.* Melbourne, AU: Methuen Australia Pty. Ltd.

Michaels, S. 1981. Sharing time: Children's narrative styles and differential access to literacy. *Language in Society,* 10, 423-442.

CHAPTER 5

Description and Details

FICTION

Description, detail, and elaboration are valued qualities of student writing. These qualities are assessed using provincial and state rubrics. Be specific, not general! Be concrete, not abstract! These recommendations abound in books and articles about writing well and developing a strong writing style. Ralph Fletcher (1993, 45) says that writers who include general information are asking their readers to "eat too high off the food chain." The 'food chain' of writing is a pyramid with a broad, general idea at the top. This idea is supported by specific, concrete details at the bottom. Fletcher goes on to explain that "writing needs to be grounded in plenty of physical details. Without them the whole food chain falls apart" (45).

As important as details are to good writing, many upper-elementary and junior-high students say that the hardest thing about writing is description and detail. Gail Lynn Goldberg and Barbara Sherr Roswell (2002) studied characteristics of girls' and boys' writing. Boys especially tended to struggle with describing and elaborating in their writing. The researchers explain that boys tend to write stories that "take the form of an undeveloped sequence of events" (93). Instruction focused on elaboration will likely not be sufficient. We must also model reading through writers' eyes whenever we read aloud to students, encouraging them to identify the concrete details that make published writers' narratives so vibrant and interesting to read. By reading well-written narratives, students can come to recognize what it means to "feed from the bottom of the food chain," and use more detail and description in their writing.

The activities in this chapter provide a starting point for students in their search for ways to elaborate on their writing. Concrete, specific detail, and strong verbs are all discussed in terms of how each can be used to help students use more detail and description in their writing.

Mini-Lesson: Using Specific Words and Phrases

Goal for Student Writers

To use specific words and expressions to enrich narrative writing.

Resources

Nathan's Story, Two Drafts of Part 1 (Fig. 5.1)
Overhead Projection, "Comparing Two Drafts of Nathan's Story" (Fig. 5.2)
Nathan's Story, Part 2 (Fig. 5.3)

Teacher and Students

In the first draft of Nathan's story (Fig. 5.1), the author underlines places where he could revise and be more specific. Part One of Nathan's story involves describing the main character, Ian, and identifying words and expressions in the story that show what Ian is like. When asked how Nathan made the second draft of his story more interesting compared to the first, students may pick out expressions such as:

"Even with his head down Ian towered over all the other twelve- and thirteen-year-olds on his team. For every year of his life Ian must have grown six inches."

These observations can be recorded on the overhead projection, "Comparing Two Drafts of Nathan's Story" (Fig. 5.2).

Students

Students should apply what they have learned about using specific words and expressions to revise Part Two of Nathan's story (Fig. 5.3) or their own writing. They can revise the underlined phrases in Nathan's story, or identify places where their own writing could be elaborated by using more specific words and expressions.

Nathan's Story: Part 1

First Draft

"I guess I have to take Ian on my team," Cass said as she chose the last player for her team.

Ian Benjamin was used to being the last one picked to play ball during lunch hour. <u>Even though he was really tall, he could never play like the other kids</u>.

His team was up to bat first, so Ian threw <u>his glove</u> down beside the bench. At least, he though his glove would land in the dirt beside the bench.

"Hey, watch where you're throwing that glove, Benjamin," Cass <u>said after Ian's glove hit her</u>.

"Great aim, Benjamin. I see you're up to your usual form," Jeff <u>said</u>.

Second Draft

"I guess I have to take Ian on my team," Cass muttered, as she chose the last player for her team.

Ian Benjamin was used to being the last one picked to play ball during lunch hour. He hadn't played much ball before he moved to Trainton, so he had a hard time keeping up to the Trainton kids. They had been playing since they could walk!

The wide, long brim of Ian's striped baseball cap hid his face as he shuffled toward the bench. Even with his head down, Ian towered over all the other twelve- and thirteen-year olds on his team. For every year of his life Ian must have grown six inches because he was close to six feet tall.

His team was up to bat first, so Ian threw his crackly-hard, new baseball glove down beside the bench. At least, he thought his glove would land in the dirt beside the bench.

"Hey, watch where you're throwing that glove, Benjamin," Cass yelled after Ian's glove deflected off the side of her face.

"Great aim, Benjamin. I see you're up to your usual form," Jeff observed.

Fig. 5.1

DESCRIPTION AND DETAILS

Comparing Two Drafts of Nathan's Story

Nathan's Drafts	How would you describe Ian?	What words and expressions has Nathan used to show you what Ian is like?
Draft #1		
Draft #1		

Fig. 5.2

GUIDED WRITING: STRATEGIES TO HELP STUDENTS BECOME BETTER WRITERS

Nathan's Story: Part 2

"Quit talking and pick up your gloves. That's three out." Cass told her team members to take their positions on the field.

Ian looked up at her for the cue to take a position, but she went to the pitcher's mound, <u>leaving him on the bench.</u> The <u>game went on</u> and the lunch hour was almost over.

"Hey Cass, you haven't let Ian play yet," Jeff said.

"Where can I put him? He throws the ball away all the time."

"How about first base? He can catch the ball," Jeff said.

Ian took first base. Greg, the first batter, <u>got to first base</u>. Jessie was up to bat. <u>Cass threw the ball and Jessie hit it.</u>

Greg went to second base, sure that it was a home run. <u>Marty caught the ball just before it went over the fence. Greg went back to first base as Marty threw the ball</u> toward first base.

"Catch that ball, Benjamin, CATCH THAT BALL," Ian said to himself. He <u>caught the ball</u> by taking one step off the base. Then he tagged the base and Greg was out!

"Benjamin, you did it!" Cass cried.

Ian <u>smiled and dropped the ball</u>.

Fig. 5.3

DESCRIPTION AND DETAILS

Mini-Lesson: Using Strong Verbs

Often, we use adjectives and adverbs to elaborate and enrich our writing. Professional writers, however, tell us that using adjectives and adverbs is not always the best way to enhance writing. Ursula Le Guin (1998), for example, recommends "a watchful attitude and a thoughtful, careful choice of adjectives and adverbs, because the bakery of English is rich beyond belief, and narrative prose, particularly if it's going a long distance, needs more muscle than fat." (62) Specific verbs provide the needed muscle.

Goal for Student Writers

To generate specific verbs to replace general verbs and then use these strong verbs in narrative writing.

Resources

Set of "Action Cards" (Fig. 5.4) for each group of three or four students in the class. These may be reproduced on card stock or construction paper and then laminated.

Teacher and Students

In small groups, students select one person to carry out the actions that are described on one of the cards. The name of the student who does the actions is used in the blank in each sentence. Another student reads the first sentence on the card. The group generates specific verbs to replace the verb and adverb in the sentence, using dictionaries or thesauri. For example, students may replace "closed the door carefully" with "nudged the door closed", or "slid the door closed." One student in the group records the specific verbs generated by the group. The new sentences are read using the more specific verbs and the actor performs the actions. Students can create new sentences with additional adverbs, as well. Students repeat the process using all the remaining sentences on the card. For the next cards, students within the group switch roles so everyone has a chance to be the reader and actor. Students post their charts and then do a carousel activity by moving in their groups from chart to chart, noting the specific verbs that each group has generated.

Students

When writing or revising their narratives, students may use these charts to help them find stronger, more descriptive verbs.

Action Cards
Using Strong Verbs
Photocopy and cut into sets of cards—
one set for each group of three or four students

_____ closed the door carefully. _____ closed the door angrily. _____ closed the door _____.	_____ held the ball carefully. _____ held the ball carelessly. _____ held the ball _____.
"Hello," _____ said loudly. "Hello," _____ said quietly. "Hello," _____ said sadly. "Hello," _____ said disgustedly. "Hello," _____ said _____.	_____ walked down the street loudly. _____ walked down the street quietly. _____ walked down the street sadly. _____ walked down the street disgustedly. _____ walked down the street _____.

Fig. 5.4

DESCRIPTION AND DETAILS

_____ took the pencil angrily.

_____ took the pencil quickly.

_____ took the pencil timidly.

_____ took the pencil confidently.

_____ took the pencil _____.

_____ hit the ball lightly.

_____ hit the ball forcefully.

_____ hit the ball timidly.

_____ hit the ball confidently.

_____ hit the ball _____.

_____ looked out the window quickly.

_____ looked out the window for a long time.

_____ looked out the window sadly.

_____ looked out the window angrily.

_____ looked out the window _____.

_____ ate the piece of cake daintily.

_____ ate the piece of cake rudely.

_____ ate the piece of cake slowly.

_____ ate the piece of cake quickly.

_____ ate the piece of cake _____.

Fig. 5.4 (cont'd)

GUIDED WRITING: STRATEGIES TO HELP STUDENTS BECOME BETTER WRITERS

Nonfiction

Detail and description are features of effective nonfiction writing. Neil W. Meriwether (1998, 200) says that concrete, specific writing has more impact than abstract writing with "vague, indefinite words and broad, general statements." While reading essays, reports, and letters, readers look for examples, explanations, comparisons and contrasts, incidents, events, and facts that support the general ideas. These detailed pieces of information at the "bottom of the food chain" help readers make sense of the bigger ideas communicated within any piece of nonfiction writing.

Providing detail in nonfiction writing is every bit as difficult as it is in fiction writing. When I read students' nonfiction writing for the Alberta provincial achievement tests over a three-year period, I observed that many students had difficulty providing the needed detail for topics that were unfamiliar to them. The strongest papers were those in which students connected the topics to specific events/ideas/facts from their own background knowledge and experience. I also found this to be true in my own classroom teaching. I observed that even after reading widely about a topic, students are better able to write descriptive nonfiction essays, reports, and letters when they have personal experience with the subject.

The teaching suggestions that follow show students how they can use information from reading and from looking at print and other media. They can talk to others, and they can use their own experiences as sources for providing specific details in their nonfiction writing.

Mini-Lesson: Giving Concrete Details to Support Big Ideas

Students can strengthen their writing by providing examples, events, quotes, and facts that are based on their own experiences and knowledge. The details anchor the big ideas in the real world and help to clarify and enrich the ideas for readers.

Goal for Student Writers

To use what they know from their own experiences and knowledge to provide concrete details of main ideas.

Resources

Nonfiction book of your choice
Overhead Projection, "Concrete Details" (Fig 5.5)

Teacher and Students

This lesson directs students to read nonfiction in order to learn about ways in which published writers provide examples and other details to support their main ideas. This is in addition to reading nonfiction to learn about the topic of the print or nonprint text. After students and their teacher read a few paragraphs from a nonfiction book, the students should identify the main ideas of the paragraphs and the concrete details that the writer uses to make each idea clear and more interesting to readers. Often, these details draw from everyday things and events. For example, in the first paragraph of the book, *Great building stories of the past*, the author writes, "in those prehistoric times, animals were greater engineers than people." (Kent 2001, 6) He then gives examples of ants, termites, wasps, birds, burrowing animals, and beavers that built mounds, nests, tunnels, and dams.

In other cases, the details might take the form of quotes from people who have experience or knowledge. The detail can also come from an incident that happens to one person and supports or extends the big idea. In the book, *Kids at work: Lewis Hine and the crusade against child labor* (1994), Freedman's main idea is that very young boys endangered their lives when they worked in Pennsylvania coal mines. He provides support through quotes, such as this one from Lewis Hine: "While I was there, two breaker boys fell or were carried into the coal chute, where they were smothered to death." (48) He also supports the idea by telling the story of Patrick Kearny, who lost his life in a mine accident in 1907, and he provides a copy of a newspaper clipping of a real incident that illustrated his main idea.

Teachers might use the overhead projection "Concrete Details" (Fig. 5.5) to record students' impressions of the main ideas and the types of supporting details in each paragraph.

Students

Students apply what they have learned about using various types of detail to support big ideas in their own nonfiction writing.

Nonfiction

Freedman, R. 1994. *Kids at work: Lewis Hine and the crusade against child labor.* New York: Clarion Books.

Kent, P. 2001. *Great building stories of the past.* Oxford, UK: Oxford University Press.

Concrete Details

Title _____

Big Idea	Details	Type of Detail

Fig. 5.5

GUIDED WRITING: STRATEGIES TO HELP STUDENTS BECOME BETTER WRITERS

© Portage and Main Press 2003. May be reproduced for classroom use. Note: photocopy at 121% for actual size

Mini-Lesson: Using Description

Ralph Fletcher and Joann Portalupi (2001) despair that students become "'compartmentalized thinkers'. . . [who] may use their powers of description while writing a narrative, but may not be aware of the value of this skill in nonfiction writing" (89). Fletcher and Portalupi argue that students need to be made aware of what sensory description can add to nonfiction writing. In this lesson, students identify how authors describe the living and nonliving things that are the subjects of their writing.

Goal for Student Writers

To use description appropriately in nonfiction writing.

Resources

Nonfiction of your choice
Overhead Projection, "Using Description in Nonfiction" (Fig. 5.6)

Teacher and Students

Published literature serves as a model for the kinds of description that are appropriate in nonfiction writing. In biographies, for example, description may be as rich and detailed as it is in fiction writing. The overhead projection, "Using Description in Nonfiction" (Fig. 5.6), can be used to record students' observations about the kinds of description that various authors use in different types of nonfiction.

Here are four examples:

In *Lucy Maud Montgomery: A Writer's Life* (2001), Elizabeth Macleod describes a few features of everyday life that contemporary readers would likely identify with:

> Life in Prince Edward Island was hard when Maud was born. There were no telephones or cars. People traveled in horse-drawn buggies on unpaved roads. Houses were cold in winter—the only heat came from wood-burning stoves and fireplaces. (6)

In *Hana's Suitcase* (2002), Karen Levine provides many details about the main character, Hana, by describing her physical appearance and her actions:

> Hana had blonde hair, blue eyes and a very pretty round face. She was a strong girl. Once in a while, Hana would provoke a battle with George, just to show off her muscles. Even though her brother was three years older, Hana would sometimes emerge the winner. But most of the time, Hana and George played well together. (15)

Science books most often describe physical details and uses or functions. In *Out of Sight: Pictures of Hidden Worlds* (2000), Seymour Simon describes tapeworms very comprehensively:

> A tapeworm is a flat worm that lives inside the digestive system of some animals, such as fishes, frogs, horses, or cows. Tapeworms are sometimes even found in people. Tapeworms can range in body length from about half an inch to thirty feet, but their heads are much smaller. This tapeworm was in the intestines of a horse. Its head has hooks that attach it to the host's intestine. A tapeworm has no mouth or digestive tract, so it absorbs food through its body surface. (unpaged)

Similarly, in his book *Great Building Stories of the Past* (2002), Peter Kent briefly describes the materials and construction of the Eiffel Tower, and how it was made. Note that similes can be very effective in nonfiction writing:

> The tower was made of iron girders, joined together by rivets. All the girders were made in Eiffel's factory, where they were joined into pieces not more than 5 metres long. These pieces were then assembled, like a giant meccano set, on the site. (29)

Students

Following a discussion about how much description is appropriate for various types of nonfiction, and the types of description that authors use in their nonfiction books, students can revise their nonfiction writing. They incorporate the level and type of descriptive detail that they feel is appropriate for the type of writing they are doing.

Nonfiction

Biography

Levine, K. 2002. *Hanas' suitcase.* Toronto: Second Story Press.
Macleod, E. 2001. *Lucy Maud Montgomery: A writer's life.* Toronto: Kids Can Press.

Science

Kent, P. 2002. *Great building stories of the past.* Oxford, UK: Oxford University Press.
Simon, S. 2000. *Out of sight: Pictures of hidden worlds.* New York: Sea Star Books.

Using Description in Nonfiction

Title of Book	Descriptive Words and Expressions	Type of Description

Fig. 5.6

DESCRIPTION AND DETAILS

REFERENCES

Fletcher, R. 1993. *What a writer needs.* Portsmouth, NH: Heinemann.

Goldberg, G. L., & Roswell, B. S. (2002). *Reading, writing and gender: Instructional strategies and classroom activities that work for girls and boys.* Poughkeepsie, NY: Eye on Education.

Le Guin, U. K. 1998. *Steering the craft: Exercises and discussions on story writing for the lone navigator or the mutinous crew.* Portland, OR: Eighth Mountain Press.

Merriwether, N. W. 1998. *Strategies for writing successful essays.* Lincolnwood, IL: NTC Publishing Group.

Portalupi, J., & Fletcher, R. 2001. *Nonfiction craft lessons: Teaching information writing K-8.* Portland, ME: Stenhouse Pub.

CHAPTER 6

Teaching Writing Conventions and Editing Skills

Sometimes the two words, *editing* and *revising* are used interchangeably to mean "fixing up" a piece of writing. In this book, **editing** means making changes to the punctuation, spelling, and grammar to conform to writing conventions considered to be "correct." **Revising** involves changes to the language, ideas, organization, tone, and all other aspects of the writing apart from spelling, punctuation, and grammar. Revising is not aimed at using correct writing conventions, but rather at clarifying and enriching the writing.

This chapter focuses on developing editing skills through teacher modelling and identifying patterns in writing. Spelling, punctuation, and grammar exercises do not develop a student's use of writing conventions as effectively as do frequent opportunities to read and write (Weaver 1996). For many students, explicit instruction is necessary because they do not pick up on the spelling, punctuation, and grammar conventions as they read, and they need someone to point them out in order to become aware of them.

This chapter begins with frequently asked questions about editing. This is followed by suggestions for student-teacher editing conferences, a template for tracking students' progress, and a mini-lesson that teaches students to use editing symbols. The final mini-lessons teach writing conventions. The overall goal in this chapter is to provide students with strategies and cues that develop their independence in the conventional uses of spelling, punctuation, and grammar.

I generally apply two types of lessons to teaching whatever spelling, grammar, and punctuation rules my students are not using correctly. The first type of lesson uses **inductive teaching.** It involves searching for examples of the spelling/punctuation/grammar rule, and then identifying the patterns to determine the rule. The other type of mini-lesson uses **deductive teaching.** It explains spelling, punctuation, or grammar rules, followed by examples of each rule. Each type of lesson culminates with students applying the rules as they write and edit.

Frequently Asked Questions about Classroom Editing

1. Should every convention error be corrected?

   That depends on the culture of your school and community. If you are in a community that expects every published piece of classroom writing to be free of convention errors before it is displayed, you will need to establish a system. This system might be one where a teacher, parent or high school work experience student, for example, does the final edit on stories to be displayed. If your community accepts convention errors in displays of student writing, then you can use one-on-one student-teacher editing conferences to teach spelling, punctuation, and grammar. This will allow you to respond to what each student's writing shows about his/her knowledge of writing conventions. Students will learn most effectively when you identify only one or two patterns of errors in their writing, and you work together to correct them.

2. How can I motivate students to edit their writing?

   After the excitement and relief of finishing a piece of writing, editing can be a dreary undertaking for many students. Knowing that their writing will be displayed in the classroom will help motivate them. Organizing a wider audience to read the work often gives students added incentive to edit their writing. You might approach local newspapers or children's magazines.

   Have students edit their work together, in pairs. This reduces the feeling of isolation, one major deterrent to students' willingness to edit. Reading a piece of writing aloud often highlights what needs to be edited. Students are more apt to recognize misspellings, missed punctuation, or awkward sentence constructions as they read aloud to someone else.

   Note: If students use word processors, editing is a less arduous task because students do not have to recopy everything they have written.

3. Should I correct grammatical errors that mirror the student's oral language?

   Often, grammatical errors reflect oral language grammar patterns used by students and members of their community. These errors are not likely to be identified by the students, nor by their peers. To show respect for students' oral language, you might tell students that although they use certain phrases in speech and friends and family understand them, they will be understood and respected by a wider audience if they use conventional spelling and grammar.

4. What role can peers and parents play in students' editing?

   Teachers do not have to be the only ones who help students edit their writing. Parents and peers can also edit students' work. This leaves the teacher to conduct student-teacher conferences and author circles. Here are some suggestions for involving peers and parents as editors.

- Each day, have a different student act as the class editor. Anyone who needs a peer editor signs up to work with the editor of the day. An editing corner or centre could be set up in the classroom with copies of References from this book, dictionaries, thesauri, spell checker books, coloured pencils, and other materials for students to use while editing.

- Pair students with an editing buddy for a period of time—a month, for example. During that time, the students confer with each other when they need editing assistance.

- During certain days of the week, have parents come into the classroom and act as editors. Students who need help may sign up to work with the parent editor on those days.

- To assess the editing abilities of your students, establish a system for editing. Students could edit using pencil or a single coloured pencil. A colour-coding system could be established where a second colour is used by peer editors, and a third colour could be used by the parent or teacher/editor.

Guiding Students' Editing: Student-Teacher Editing Conferences

Conferences can be held for several purposes. They can be useful for guiding students' editing, or for helping with the content of their writing. Student-teacher conferences are also valuable teaching and assessment tools. During the five- to ten-minute one-on-one editing conference, teachers can gather information about the student's abilities to identify and correct convention errors. The conference is an ideal setting for individual instruction that is based on the student's writing.

The assessment checklist, "Student-Teacher Editing Conference Record" (Fig. 6.1), is useful for recording information and tracking students' progress in their use of writing conventions and the editing process. Teachers who need an example of the conference record should refer to "Student-Teacher Editing Conference Record, example" for guidance. (Fig. 6.2)

Here is one way to carry out an editing conference:

1. Read the piece of writing, and determine the types of errors the student has made (e.g., using apostrophes after the "s" in plural nouns that are not possessive, confusing homonyms, punctuating dialogue incorrectly).

2. Select one or two types of errors that are repeated throughout the writing, and compare the errors to the conventional forms.

3. Ask the student to look for other examples of these errors and edit the writing.

4. The student shows the teacher the edited writing and then writes the final draft of the story.

Student-Teacher Editing Conference Record

Student's Name _____

Date/Title of Student Writing	Types of Convention Errors Identified	Teacher's Comments

Fig. 6.1

GUIDED WRITING: STRATEGIES TO HELP STUDENTS BECOME BETTER WRITERS

Student-Teacher Editing Conference Record • Example

Student's Name Ashoak

Date/Title of Student Writing	Types of Convention Errors Identified	Teacher's Comments
Sept. 30	• possession • punctuation in dialogue • quotation marks	• often omits the apostrophe • rarely uses commas to separate dialogue from rest of sentence I showed Ashoak examples of both of these errors and asked him to focus on them when editing his next story. • uses these fairly consistently now
Oct. 19 The Mercury Monster	• punctuation in dialogue • possession	• uses commas quite often • still having problems differentiating plural and possessive nouns—pointed out the differences using examples from his story
December 12 Prize Money	• punctuation in dialogue • possession • capitalization of brand names, streets, and names of characters	• uses commas quite often • uses apostrophe in possessive nouns most of the time • focused on this today—will have mini lesson next week because others are having problems also

Fig. 6.2

TEACHING WRITING CONVENTIONS AND EDITING SKILLS

Mini-Lesson: Using Editing Symbols

Students who are aware of the editing symbols used by professional editors have the tools they need to become more independent in the process of editing their own writing. This lesson introduces editing symbols and provides unedited writing samples for students to practice using editing symbols.

Goal for Student Writers

To have students recognize and use editing symbols when editing.

Resources

Chart, "Editing Symbols" (Fig. 6.3)
Overhead Projection, "Ashoak's Story, Part 1" (Fig. 6.4)
Overhead Projection, "Ashoak's Story, Part 2" (Fig. 6.5)

Teacher and Students

Editing symbols help students identify the following types of changes to written work:

- inserting punctuation marks, letters, or words
- deleting punctuation marks, letters, or words
- changing letters from upper case to lower case
- identifying misspelled words
- indenting for new speakers or new paragraphs

Students can consult figure 6.3 to learn which symbols are used by professional editors to identify each type of editorial change. The overhead projection, "Ashoak's Story, Part 1" (Fig. 6.4) can be used for guided practice in using the symbols.

Students

Students can practice using editing symbols with "Ashoak's Story, Part 2" (Fig 6.5), or they can edit their own writing.

Editing Symbols

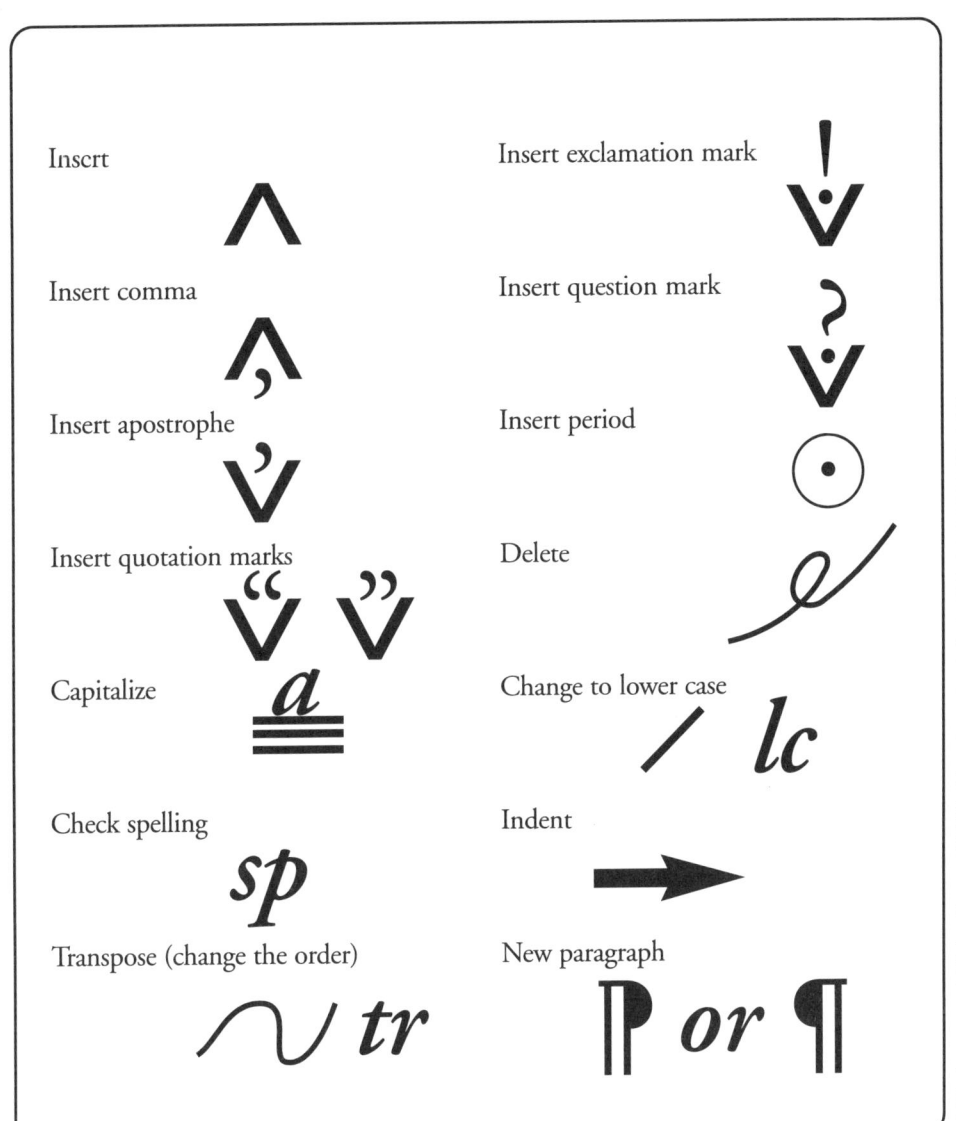

Insert	∧	Insert exclamation mark	!∨
Insert comma	∧,	Insert question mark	?∨
Insert apostrophe	∨'	Insert period	⊙
Insert quotation marks	∨" ∨"	Delete	*(delete symbol)*
Capitalize	*a* (underlined thrice)	Change to lower case	/ *lc*
Check spelling	*sp*	Indent	→
Transpose (change the order)	∽ *tr*	New paragraph	¶ or ¶

Fig. 6.3

TEACHING WRITING CONVENTIONS AND EDITING SKILLS

Overhead Projection

Ashoak's Story, Part 1

Professor Abdalkhani head of the biotecnology department locked the door of his office. He glanced quickly over his shoulder dropped the key in his pocket and darted down the back stiars. At the bottom of the stairs, the professor tripped and fell at the feet of izzy m sinister (initials I. M. Sinister). The professor gasped. When he saw his son Ali bound and gagged behind the stair well.

"So professor Abdalkhani, you thought you could escape me, Izzy snarled

"Let my son go he has no part in your sinister plot. The public needs to know of the dangers of your new pizza crust"" professor Abdalkhani began.

"It is an ingeneus recipe" Izzy bragged "a pizza crust that forms it's own tomato sauce and up to five toppings as it bakes."

"But it also forms ulcers in peoples stomachs," the professor protested. "My report shows that eight out of ten people had painful ulcer attacks after eating your pizzas for a month."

Fig. 6.4

Overhead Projection

Ashoak's Story, Part 2

Izzy wasn't listening he was thinking only of the money he would make selling the revolutionary pizza crusts.

"Now give me that report. If you want your son to live to see his grandchildren you will give it to me now," Izzys voice rose to a shout and he shook his knife blade in front of professor Abdalkhani's face. "Will you let my son go" the professor asked as he fished around in his pockets for the pages of the report.

Izzy grabbed his hand and ripped open the professor's pocket a blizzard of papers blew around him. He greedily gathered up the papers. Just then the emergency exit door opend and detective Bends yelled, "Drop that knife and trun around slowly Mr. Sinister. We've had enough of your games for today." The detective handcufed izzy and the professor used Izzys knife to cut the ropes around his sons hands.

"I thought you would never show up," Professor Abdalkhani said to the detective.

We came over as soon as we got your call but we couldn't get this emergency door open from the outside. we had to take the hinges off," the Detective replied. "Thanks to you the izzy pizza crust will never go on the market. You've saved millions of people from geting ulcers"

"Thats my job, detective," Professor Abdalkhani said with a smile. He and his son followed the detective out the door and went home.

Fig. 6.5

Using Inductive Teaching:
Look for Patterns Across Specific Examples

Mini-Lesson: Punctuating Dialogue

Using speech in narrative writing may be a struggle for young writers. There are many variations on the placement of dialogue within a sentence, and this makes using capital letters, commas, and end punctuation complicated. In this inductive lesson, students choose examples of dialogue in books and examine the patterns in the use of punctuation. They then generalize the rules for punctuating dialogue.

Goal for Student Writers

To understand punctuation rules for dialogue that comes at the beginning, middle (interrupted), and end of a sentence.

Resources

Template, "Punctuating Dialogue" (Fig. 6.6)
Overhead Projection, "Writing the Rules: Punctuating Dialogue" (Fig. 6.7)
Published children's literature

Teacher and Students

To gain a greater awareness of the use of punctuation in dialogue, students search through published fiction and biography. They can identify examples of dialogue that occur at the beginning, in the middle (interrupted), and at the end of sentences. After students write the examples in the appropriate place on the template, "Punctuating Dialogue" (Fig. 6.6), they write an explanation of the rules for using capital letters, commas, and other punctuation in dialogue.

Note: The grey bars in the examples separate the dialogue from the rest of the sentence to highlight the three positions in the sentence.

Students should share the rules with the rest of the class. The teacher should use the overhead projection, "Writing the Rules: Punctuating Dialogue" (Fig. 6.7) to confirm the students' observations. Students can then reinforce their use of punctuation in dialogue by editing their own writing or their peers' writing.

Students

Students apply the rules for punctuating dialogue in their own writing.

Punctuating Dialogue

Instructions

Find examples of dialogue in books you are reading. Write the examples in the appropriate section of this page, depending on whether the dialogue is at the beginning, at the end, or is interrupted in the middle of a sentence.

At the Beginning
"The clock is chiming midnight and you're stepping on my glass slipper, oh handsome prince," Cinderella observed.
Other Examples: _____
_____
_____
_____
_____
_____

Interrupted
"What she means," Cinderella's coach driver sneered, "is that she wants you to get off her foot, you clumsy ox."
Other Examples: _____
_____
_____
_____
_____
_____

At the End
The prince blushed and stammered, "So sorry. I thought I saw a fairy godmother sitting on Cinderella's shoulder pointing her to watch. I lost my footing."
Other Examples: _____
_____
_____
_____
_____
_____

Fig. 6.6

Writing the Rules: Punctuating Dialogue

At the Beginning
"The clock is chiming midnight and you're stepping on my glass slipper, oh handsome prince," Cinderella observed.
Punctuation Rule: _____
_____
_____
_____
_____

Interrupted
"What she means," Cinderella's coach driver sneered, "is that she wants you to get off her foot, you clumsy ox."
Punctuation Rule: _____
_____
_____
_____
_____

At the End
The prince blushed and stammered, "So sorry. I thought I saw a fairy godmother sitting on Cinderella's shoulder pointing to her watch. I lost my footing."
Punctuation Rule: _____
_____
_____
_____
_____

Fig. 6.7

Using Deductive Teaching: Learning the Rule and Finding Examples

Mini-Lesson: Capitalization Rules

Although most English spelling rules have exceptions, there are some spelling generalizations, such as those for capitalization, that are regularly applied with few or no exceptions (Thomas 1979, 68). It is worthwhile spending time teaching these rules directly. This mini-lesson teaches the rules deductively by introducing a set of rules and then engaging students in a BINGO game, where they identify rules that are followed and those that are broken.

Goal for Student Writers

To use capital letters correctly when using names, titles, abbreviations, and 'I' in their writing.

Resources

Poster, "Uses of Capital Letters" (Fig. 6.8), with examples of words that are capitalized
"Create a Card: Capitalization Rules for BINGO Squares" (Fig. 6.9)
"Capitalization BINGO Card" (Fig. 6.10)
"Capitalization BINGO Card: Teacher's Game Card" (Fig. 6.11)
Overhead Projection, "Buried Treasure in Cutthroat Cave" (Fig. 6.12)

Teacher and Students

In this deductive lesson, the teacher uses the poster, "Uses of Capital Letters" (Fig. 6.8) or other resources to introduce students to rules for capitalizing names, titles, abbreviations, and "I." Students apply the rules in a BINGO game. In the game, students read a narrative in which some words are capitalized correctly and others are not. They then edit the writing and identify which rule applies.

To create their BINGO cards, students cut out the capitalization rule squares from "Create a Card: Capitalization Rules for BINGO Squares" (Fig. 6.9) and glue them randomly onto the blank "Capitalization BINGO Card" (Fig. 6.10). Each square must have a rule on it. A rule can appear more than once on a card and more than once in any column. Teachers will want to use the "Capitalization BINGO Card: Teacher's Game Card" during the game (Fig. 6.11).

The BINGO game involves reading the narrative on the overhead projection, "Buried Treasure in Cutthroat Cave" (Fig. 6.12), one sentence at a time. Students identify whether names, titles, abbreviations, and "I" have been used correctly. The student or teacher edits the writing with an erasable pen. The students then identify the capitalization rule that applies. The teacher calls one of the letters in BINGO.

If the student's card has a square with that capitalization rule, the student places the BINGO chip or other marker on one square. The teacher keeps a record of capitalization rules that have been used under each letter on the "Capitalization BINGO Card: Teacher's Game Card." The game continues until a winner has been declared, or until the story is completely edited.

Students

Students apply the capitalization rules when editing their writing.

Uses of Capital Letters

1. **Titles:** first word, last word, and all other words except for articles, prepositions, and conjunctions
   People in my Life

2. **The word "I"**
   I am Frances Hamilton. Stay tuned, and I will introduce myself and the people in my life.

3. **Days of the week and months of the year**
   I was born on a Wednesday in February 1987.

4. **Names of people and animals**
   My brothers' names are Mark and Carl. My dog's name is Spud.

5. **Titles given to people when the titles appear before the person's name**
   My mom is a pastor. People call her Pastor Hamilton.

6. **Names of companies or businesses and brand names**
   My brother works at Mickey's Pizza Place.

7. **Names of streets, avenues, boulevards, etc.**
   We live on Elida Road.

8. **Names of towns, provinces, states, countries**
   We live in Moonbeam, Manitoba, Canada. Our cousins live in Crooked Creek, Montana, United States.

9. **Abbreviations that appear before a name, such as Mr., Ms., Dr.**
   My teacher's name is Mr. Laroiya, and my principal's name is Ms. Bellefontaine.

10. **Names of holidays and events**
    Last Halloween my mom bought me a pet snake. I brought my snake to school for Show and Tell.

11. **Names of languages, nationalities, and religious groups**
    We speak English at home. My Vietnamese friend, Tuyet, speaks Vietnamese at home.

Fig. 6.8

Create a Card • Capitalization Rules for BINGO Squares

Directions: Cut out the squares on this page. Glue squares randomly on the blank BINGO card. You may use each rule more than once on your BINGO card and more than once in any column.

names of people and animals	days of the week, months of the year	for the word "I"	titles: first, last, and all other words except articles, prepositions, conjunctions	names of languages, nationalities, religious groups
names of people and animals	days of the week, months of the year	for the word "I"	titles: first, last, and all other words except articles, prepositions, conjunctions	names of languages, nationalities, religious groups
names of people and animals	days of the week, months of the year	for the word "I"	names of towns, provinces, states, countries	names of languages, nationalities, religious groups
names of people and animals	names of streets, avenues, boulevards, etc.	names of companies, businesses, brands	names of towns, provinces, states, countries	names of holidays and special events
abbreviations such as Mr., Mrs., Ms., Dr.	names of streets, avenues, boulevards, etc.	names of companies, businesses, brands	names of towns, provinces, states, countries	names of holidays and special events
abbreviations such as Mr., Mrs., Ms., Dr.	names of streets, avenues, boulevards, etc.	names of companies, businesses, brands	names of languages, nationalities, religious groups	names of holidays and special events
abbreviations such as Mr., Mrs., Ms., Dr.	for the word "I"	titles given to people when titles appear before the person's name	titles given to people when titles appear before the person's name	titles given to people when titles appear before the person's name

Fig. 6.9

GUIDED WRITING: STRATEGIES TO HELP STUDENTS BECOME BETTER WRITERS

Capitalization BINGO Card

Directions: Cut out this card on the dotted lines. Glue the squares with capitalization rules randomly on this card. You may use each rule more than once on your BINGO card, and more than once in any column.

B	I	N	G	O
		FREE		

Fig. 6.10

© Portage and Main Press 2003. May be reproduced for classroom use. Note: photocopy at 121% for actual size

TEACHING WRITING CONVENTIONS AND EDITING SKILLS

Capitalization BINGO Card
Teacher's Game Card

B	I	N	G	O
names of languages, nationalities, religious groups	names of languages, nationalities, religious groups	names of languages, nationalities, religious groups	names of languages, nationalities, religious groups	names of languages, nationalities, religious groups
titles: first, last, and all other words except articles, prepositions, conjunctions	titles: first, last, and all other words except articles, prepositions, conjunctions	titles: first, last, and all other words except articles, prepositions, conjunctions	titles: first, last, and all other words except articles, prepositions, conjunctions	titles: first, last, and all other words except articles, prepositions, conjunctions
for the word "I"	for the word "I"	for the word "I"	for the word "I"	for the word "I"
names of people and animals	names of people and animals	names of people and animals	names of people and animals	names of people and animals
names of holidays and special events	names of holidays and special events	names of holidays and special events	names of holidays and special events	names of holidays and special events
names of towns, provinces, states, countries	names of towns, provinces, states, countries	names of towns, provinces, states, countries	names of towns, provinces, states, countries	names of towns, provinces, states, countries
names of companies, businesses, brand names	names of companies, businesses, brand names	names of companies, businesses, brand names	names of companies, businesses, brand names	names of companies, businesses, brand names
titles given to people titles appear before the person's name	titles given to people titles appear before the person's name	titles given to people titles appear before the person's name	titles given to people titles appear before the person's name	titles given to people titles appear before the person's name
days of the week, months of the year	days of the week, months of the year	days of the week, months of the year	days of the week, months of the year	days of the week, months of the year
abbreviations such as Mr., Mrs., Ms., Dr.	abbreviations such as Mr., Mrs., Ms., Dr.	abbreviations such as Mr., Mrs., Ms., Dr.	abbreviations such as Mr., Mrs., Ms., Dr.	abbreviations such as Mr., Mrs., Ms., Dr.
names of streets, avenues, etc.	names of streets, avenues, etc.	names of streets, avenues, etc.	names of streets, avenues, etc.	names of streets, avenues, etc.

Fig. 6.11

Buried treasure in cutthroat Cave

My name is Horace marauder. People know me only as captain Horace.

I sail the atlantic ocean in my vessel, the dolly searobber, with my first mate, johnny buccaneer.

We picked up the rest of the crew in Portugal, Spain and france last september.

I got started in the pirate business after a deal with the purloiner brothers of the fishmonger trading company went sour.

Before Thursday, march 17, 1904, i was an honest business man living in boston, massachusetts.

After that day, I vowed to get revenge for the murder of my brother, the honorable doctor, Boris marauder, and for the theft of the marauder family fortune.

With my trusty bull terrier, halibut, at my side, I left my modest home on patent street, swearing that I would return when the purloiner brothers had paid for my brother's murder and i had the family fortune back in my hands.

Halibut, johnny, and I have been on the seas since that fateful st. patrick's day in 1904.

In the past three years, we've learned three languages, portuguese, spanish and french—as we worked with our new crew. But that's not all.

We've been the terror of the atlantic for ships carrying goods sold by the fishmonger trading company.

The purloiner brothers are having difficulty finding captains to command their merchant vessels. The word is out that pirate horace is targeting their shipments.

The purloiner brothers sent a telegram last Wednesday demanding to meet me by friday.

I sent the purloiner brothers a book called "diary of a sailor stranded on Cutthroat Island" and a message that they were to meet me at cutthroat cave at 1500 hours on Friday.

Friday was a blustery day. I rowed in from the dolly searobber with my scuba diving suit and halibut stowed in the bottom of the scow, and two muskets under my coat.

The purloiner brothers were there with their scow tied to a stone on the beach. I could see two of their hit men crouching behind the only other rock on the flat, treeless island.

Fig. 6.12

I tied up my scow next to theirs and halibut snuck out to start gnawing at the ropes of the purloiners' scow.

"We should have known that captain horace was really horace marauder. At last we have a chance to repay you for all that you have done for us these past three years," bert purloiner smirked.

"You don't think I'd let you get rid of me that easily, do you?" i fingered the muskets under my coat and kept my eyes on the two hit men. I knew that the purloiners never carried weapons.

The flash of steel from behind the rock told me I had no time to lose. I fired my muskets. My years as a pirate had sharpened my aim and I dropped both hit men before they had time to pull the triggers.

Fear simmered in the purloiner brothers' eyes. They could see their scow floating out into the atlantic—Halibut had done her job well—and their hit men lying dead beside the rock.

"Now it's my turn to repay you for all that you have done to my family," I warned. "If you want to come out of this alive, you must sign this paper giving my family back the money you stole in the st. patrick's day deal of 1904. It also says that you are responsible for the death of my brother."

"Anything. We'll do anything you say," the purloiner brothers groveled. Bert signed the statement as president bert purloiner and his brother signed as vice-president benjamin purloiner.

"Thank you. It's been great doing business with you. Now my faithful halibut and I must be on our way. We have appointments to keep back on patent avenue," I aimed my muskets at the two, defying them to follow me into my scow.

"But what about us? You said you would help us," the purloiner brothers blubbered.

"I'll send in shipments to see that you don't starve or die from exposure, care of the fishmonger trading company. After a few months, someone might figure out where you are and rescue you. I might even do it myself if a benevolent mood hits me."

I took a box from my scow and pushed it in the purloiners' direction. "Here's your first shipment. It should hold you for a month or so."

I untied the scow, keeping my muskets pointed at the purloiner brothers, and settled in to row halibut and myself back to the dolly searobber.

When i returned to boston, I paid the crew handsomely for their work with me. Then, I settled back into routine as a businessman.

As for the purloiners, I had been sending them monthly shipments, but they don't want them anymore. They started a business on the island; purloiners' dune buggy rides.

Fig. 6.12 (cont'd)
GUIDED WRITING: STRATEGIES TO HELP STUDENTS BECOME BETTER WRITERS

Mini-Lesson: Identifying and Transforming Sentence Fragments

While sentence fragments can be used effectively to communicate a certain effect, image, or emotion, unintentional use of fragments by young writers results in writing that is difficult to follow. Understanding independent clauses, dependent clauses, and phrases helps students recognize and avoid writing fragments.

Goals for Student Writers
- To recognize three ways that sentence fragments are usually created.
- To think of ways to create complete sentences from sentence fragments.

Resources

Overhead Projection, "Sentence Fragments: Subordinating Conjunctions" (Fig. 6.13)
Overhead Projection, "Sentence Fragments: Prepositional Phrases" (Fig. 6.14)
Overhead Projection, "Sentence Fragments: Noun Phrases" (Fig. 6.15)
Overhead Projection, "Savani's Story, Part 1" (Fig. 6.16)
Overhead Projection, "Savani's Story, Part 2" (Fig. 6.17)

Teacher and Students

In this deductive lesson, the teacher uses examples from the overhead projections provided to introduce students to three ways in which fragments are created. The examples show how fragments are created when writers:
- place subordinating conjunctions ("before" or "since") in front of a complete sentence
- separate a prepositional phrase from the rest of the sentence
- isolate phrases that can replace the noun in a previous sentence

The examples also show how the fragments can easily be made into complete sentences. The next step is to apply the knowledge about how fragments are created and how they can be made into complete sentences through editing. "Savani's Story, Part 1" can be used for guided practice.

Students

Students edit "Savani's Story, Part 2" (Fig. 6.17) or their own writing.

Sentence Fragments
Subordinating Conjunctions

Sometimes writers create sentence fragments by placing subordinating conjunctions in front of sentences:

> Before David got his motorbike. He rode his bicycle to basketball practice every Thursday night. David has been late for every basketball practice. Since he started riding his new motorbike.

To create complete sentences from these fragments, you can combine the fragment and the sentence it refers to:

> Before David got his motorbike, he rode his bicycle to basketball practice every Thursday night. David has been late for every basketball practice since he started riding his new motorbike.

Common Subordinating Conjunctions

Cause: since, because, as, so that
Condition: if, whether, unless
Contrast: although, rather than, whereas, until, after
Time: as, while, before, since, when

Fig. 6.13

Sentence Fragments
Prepositional Phrases

Sometimes writers create sentence fragments by separating prepositional phrases from the rest of the sentence:

> Lately David gets to basketball practice. [About ten minutes late]. He has trouble getting his motorbike started so he leaves it running. [In the parking lot outside the gym].

To create complete sentences from these fragments, you can combine the prepositional phrase with the sentence:

> Lately David gets to basketball practice about ten minutes late. He has trouble getting his motorbike started so he leaves it running in the parking lot outside the gym.

Examples of Prepositional Phrases

Time: by noon, at two o'clock, around two o'clock, after lunch
Place: to basketball practice, at the school, around the corner, on the street

© Portage and Main Press 2003. May be reproduced for classroom use.
Note: photocopy at 121% for actual size

Fig. 6.14

TEACHING WRITING CONVENTIONS AND EDITING SKILLS

Sentence Fragments
Noun Phrases

Sometimes writers create sentence fragments by leaving noun phrases that can replace another noun (appositives) on their own:

> David tells the coach about his problems with the **battery**. The one he bought from a friend for five dollars. The coach gives David a disapproving **look**. The kind that makes David think he should start riding his bike again.

To create complete sentences from these fragments, combine the noun phrase (e.g., "the one he bought from a friend for five dollars") with the noun it refers to (e.g., "the battery"). You will probably need to use a comma to separate the two.

> David tells the coach about his problems with the battery, the one he bought from a friend for five dollars. The coach gives David a disapproving look, the kind that makes David think he should start riding his bike again.

Fig. 6.15

Savani's Story, Part 1

Keltie burst through the door. In her muddy dress, socks, and shoes. Her knobby knees peeked out under a dress. That looked like it had been worn in a mud wrestling competition.

She shook her hair out of her eyes and two stringy hair ribbons dropped onto the floor. Keltie grabbed the ribbons and stuck them back in her hair. "Stupid ribbons. I told mom I didn't need these ratty old things."

Nine-year old Keltie flipped her shoes. Into a corner of the porch and ran into the kitchen. Her mom's eyes popped out of her head. When she saw Keltie's muddy dress and socks.

Fig. 6.16

Savani's Story, Part 2

"Don't touch ANYTHING before I get you cleaned up. Take your socks off and follow me to the bathroom."

Keltie's bare feet squeeched on the linoleum. As she headed for the bathroom.

Her younger sister, Tara, toddled in. With her teddy bear to see what would happen next. "Dir-ty, dir-ty," she said.

Keltie's green eyes flashed. As she grabbed her baby sister's teddy and threw it into the bathtub. Before her mom could stop her. Keltie turned on the water.

"Keltie, why did you do that?" her mom demanded. As she squeezed the water out of the bear.

"Teddy needs a bath, too," Keltie said innocently.

Her mom sighed. She held out the green dress that Keltie's grandma had bought Keltie last week. "Your grandmother expects this dress to be clean for her birthday."

Neither Keltie nor her mom expected the dress to be clean, but they would be surprised how dirty it would be by the end of the day.

Fig. 6.17

REFERENCES

Thomas, V. 1979. *Teaching spelling.* 2nd Ed. Toronto: Gage.

Weaver, C. 1996. *Teaching grammar in context.* Portsmouth, NH: Heinemann.